Chinese-English edition
中 英 文 对 照

SUN-TZU:
THE ART OF WARFARE

孙子兵法

李零 今译　　[美] 安乐哲 英译

Translated by

Li Ling (Modern Chinese)

Roger T. Ames (English)

中华书局
ZHONGHUA BOOK COMPANY

SUN – TZU：THE ART OF WARFARE by Roger T. Ames
Published by arrangement with Ballantine Books，
an imprint of the Random House Publishing Group，
a division of Random House，Inc.

图书在版编目(CIP)数据

孙子兵法：汉英对照/(春秋)孙武著；李零今译；
(美)安乐哲(Ames，R.)英译.—北京：中华书局，2012.6
  ISBN 978 – 7 – 101 – 08803 – 8

  Ⅰ.孙…　Ⅱ.①孙…②李…③安…　Ⅲ.兵法 – 中国 –
春秋时代 – 汉、英　Ⅳ.E892.25

  中国版本图书馆 CIP 数据核字(2012)第 161998 号

书　　名	孙子兵法(中英文对照)
今 译 者	李　零
英 译 者	〔美〕安乐哲(Roger Ames)
责任编辑	张继海
出版发行	中华书局
	(北京市丰台区太平桥西里 38 号　100073)
	http://www.zhbc.com.cn
	E – mail：zhbc@ zhbc.com.cn
印　　刷	北京市白帆印务有限公司
版　　次	2012 年 6 月北京第 1 版
	2012 年 6 月北京第 1 次印刷
规　　格	开本/787 × 1092 毫米　1/32
	印张 5½　插页 2　字数 80 千字
印　　数	1 – 10000 册
国际书号	ISBN 978 – 7 – 101 – 08803 – 8
定　　价	20.00 元

钱德明（Jean-Joseph-Marie Amiot, 1718~1793）
法国汉学家，把《孙子兵法》介绍到欧洲的第一人

前　言

李　零

　　谢谢张夕，感谢他把我的白话译文和安乐哲教授的英文译文，剪辑并列，做成双语对照的读本，让大家对《孙子兵法》有一种新的阅读享受。

　　《四库全书总目》说，《孙子兵法》是"百代谈兵之祖"。这是清代学者总结历代兵书得出的评语。其实，它不仅是咱们中国的兵学经典，也是全世界的兵学经典。

　　正如大家已经了解到的，早在公元8世纪，此书就已传入日本。18世纪，由法国耶稣会的传教士钱德明翻译，《孙子》还传入欧洲。如今，它有几十种不同语言的译本，影响遍及全世界。中国古书在世界有名，这书在前三名之内。

　　至于中文的白话译本，早在1944年，郭化若将军在延安就已出版过《白话译解孙子兵法》。1949年后，白话译本如雨后春笋，不仅郭化若将军出过修订本，其他译本也多得不得了。

　　我们的译本只是众多译本中的两种。它们都是辅助材料，目的是为了帮大家读这部兵法本身。

军事是国之大事，人类最先进的科学技术，最先进的组织手段，总是率先投入其中。就连人琢磨人互相斗心眼的学问也属它发达。它不仅是技术，也是艺术。

《孙子》的《虚实》篇有一句名言，"兵无常势，水无常形"。我用一句粗俗的话来传递其精神，叫"唯一的规则，就是没有规则"。

战争，千头万绪，瞬息万变，最难捕捉其规律。人类打了几千年的仗，血流成河，泪流成河，赢了是宝贵经验，输了是惨痛教训，事后总结可以，但没人卖后悔药。古今中外，多少人绞尽脑汁，谁不想参透其中的玄机？你要知道，中国出了本《孙子兵法》，这事可不容易呀。

西方，古典时代没有像样的兵书（只有讲战史的书），中世纪也没有。19世纪以前，没有一部兵书可以同它相比。利德尔·哈特说，要比只有一本，就是19世纪克劳塞维茨的《战争论》。这话丝毫也不夸大。特别是我们不要忘了，和大部头的《战争论》相比，《孙子》写得十分精炼。它是在那么古老的时代，用那么短的篇幅，对高度对抗下的应变思维，做如此透彻的分析，如此高度的概括，真可谓曲尽其妙。

人类思维的常态，绝大多数都不是在预设的静止状态下思维，更不是一厢情愿的单向思维。从这个意义上讲，我们甚至可以说，它也是一部探讨人类思维特点的经典。不仅军人应该读，所有人都值得读。

《老子》说："为学日益，为道日损。"经典的魅力是言简意赅，常读常新。它为无数读者的想象力留下了充分的思考余地。我读《孙子》读了几十年，每次读，都有新的收获。

《孙子》一书，篇幅不大，古本只有五千多字，今本只有约六千字，粗粗浏览一遍，似乎用不了太多时间。但这是一本年深月久的书，其中有许多生僻字眼，不抠不明白。对一般读者来说，不注释，不翻译，理解起来还是相当困难。

翻译是以注释为基础，注释不容易，翻译也不容易。翻译不仅可以弥补注释的不足，还能提供连贯的思索，很有用。好的注释和好的翻译，彼此是相得益彰。

白话翻译可以拉近我们和古代的距离。

英文翻译可以拉近我们和世界的距离。

近代以来，中国融入世界，有天翻地覆的大变化，汉语也不例外。现代汉语包含很多外来语，无论自然科学，还是社会科学，甚至人文学术和文学创作。我们的言谈话语、笔墨辞章，自觉不自觉，到处都渗透着外来影响。其实，不管你是否掌握外语，你的思维和语言都不可避免地置身于双语比较或多语比较之中。白话和外语，并非风马牛不相及。

前　言

　　我想，对年轻一代的读者，双语阅读是一种很好的体验。

　　祝大家阅读愉快！

　　　　　　　　2012年6月24日写于北京蓝旗营寓所

Preface to the Bilingual Edition

Roger T. Ames, University of Hawai' i

Let me first say that it is an unparalleled honor for me to have my English translation of the *Sunzi* included in a bilingual edition together with the modern Chinese rendering by Professor Li Ling, perhaps the foremost *Sunzi* scholar of our time.

We know from early court bibliographies that the *Sunzi* literature circulated broadly during the formative period leading up to Chinese empire. And from an aggregating commentarial tradition in which *Sunzi* retained its canonical status across the centuries of imperial China we can appreciate the importance of this classical text for the evolving Chinese identity. In the modern history of the sinitic Asia of China, Korea, Japan, and Vietnam, the *Sunzi* has been appealed to as a reference point for shaping a prosecuting effective strategies on the many battlefields of modern life, from familiar military applications to the more innovative arenas of Olympic sports,

Preface to the Bilingual Edition

international political negotiations, and business management. And today *Sunzi* has taken its place as a vital resource in anticipating the enrichment of traditional Western philosophy and culture in its evolving relationship with Asian cultural practices.

What has given *Sunzi* this perennial value as a heuristic for organizing the human experience broadly is not simply its wisdom on how to make the best out of a bad situation. Consistent with the persistent cosmology that is summarized in the Great Commentary of the *Book of Changes*, *Sunzi* provides us with counsel on how to coordinate human culture within its cosmic context to optimize the creative possibilities available in any situation in such a way as to make the most of the opportunity to live a human life.

Over the past generation, scholars have come to a new awareness of how the life–and–death intensity of warfare had a dramatic affect on the patterns of thinking and living that emerged in the formative years of the Chinese cultural narrative. During the centuries leading up to the state of Qin's consolidation of power on the central plains of present–day China, the ferocity and horror of internecine warfare rose exponentially. Indeed, death itself had become a way of life, and warfare had become a defining human activity in the articulation of the distinctive correlative worldview of ancient China.

Preface to the Bilingual Edition

There is a key to understanding *Sunzi* that is made available by reflecting on one of its central terms. Central to both military philosophy and life generally is the perception that any particular event is sponsored by a fluid calculus of factors captured in the idea—*shi* 势—a term that defies translation into the linear causality freighted into the English language. *Shi* describes the continuing dynamic of all of the factors that are at play in any particular situation: circumstances, configuration, momentum, authority, propensity, timing, force, leverage, weight, velocity, precision, a triggering device, and so on, that can be coordinated and calibrated to achieve relational advantage. Importantly, this notion of *shi* was initially a key military vocabulary connoting the strategic advantage or "purchase" that is achieved relative to the enemy through exploiting differentials in information, terrain, morale, training, numbers, supplies, weaponry, and so on.

In the military texts *shi* has been captured with different images: the power of the crossbow bolt controlled from a tiny trigger but able to pierce an enemy from a distance that itself serves as protection, the unstoppable force of round logs and boulders thundering down a steep ravine, a bird of prey swooping down and striking another animal out of the sky.

Preface to the Bilingual Edition

Shi, a fundamentally aesthetic notion, is "compositional" in at least two senses: self and other are coterminous and mutually entailing, thus making available the possibility of "com–positioning" and thus reconfiguring the situation to one's advantage. We are able to redefine ourselves and our situation by coordinating shared relations and replacing the present configuration of relations to precipitate an advantage on one side at the expense of the other. Strategically we can seek inspiration in the reconfiguring dyadic pairs such as far and near (*jinyuan* j 近远), strong and weak (*qiangruo* 强弱), large and small (*daxiao* 大小), regular and irregular attacks (*zhengqi* 正奇), vital and tangential assets (*qingzhong* 轻重), arrogance and humility (*jiaobei* 骄卑), concentrated and dispersed (*zhuansan* 专散), offensive and defensive postures (*gongshou* 攻守), wisdom and stupidity (*zhiyu* 智愚), taking and giving (取予), victory and defeat (*shengbai* 胜败), and so on.

This correlative strategy for understanding and influencing a situation is fundamentally aesthetic, requiring as a first step the full consideration of all of the details that produce the totality of the present, actual effect. This holism means that the *Sunzi* is not simply a text that teaches its reader success in finite games—that is, the strategies and tactics that enable one side in a dialectical en-

Preface to the Bilingual Edition

gagement to manipulate the propensity of circumstances to take the victory. More importantly, the *Sunzi* is ultimately about infinite games that do not end with one side winning and the other side losing. Infinite games—the inclusive games that we play in family and community—are played to strengthen the relationships that obtain in any situation, enabling us thereby to not only restore harmony in the world, but also to reset the conditions in such a way as to provide an opportunity for shared human flourishing.

目录

计第一 …………………………………………………………………… 2

作战第二………………………………………………………………… 12

谋攻第三………………………………………………………………… 22

形第四…………………………………………………………………… 32

势第五…………………………………………………………………… 40

虚实第六………………………………………………………………… 50

军争第七………………………………………………………………… 64

九变第八………………………………………………………………… 76

行军第九………………………………………………………………… 84

地形第十………………………………………………………………… 104

九地第十一……………………………………………………………… 118

火攻第十二……………………………………………………………… 142

用间第十三……………………………………………………………… 150

CONTENTS

Chapter 1: On Assessments ·································· 3

Chapter 2: On Waging Battle ······························ 13

Chapter 3: Planning the Attack ························· 23

Chapter 4: Strategic Positions (Hsing) ·············· 33

Chapter 5: Strategic Advantage (Shih) ············· 41

Chapter 6: Weak Points and Strong Points ·········· 51

Chapter 7: Armed Contest ······························· 65

Chapter 8: Adapting to the Nine Contingencies (pien) ··· 77

Chapter 9: Deploying the Army ························ 85

Chapter 10: The Terrain ······························ 105

Chapter 11: The Nine Kinds of Terrain ·············· 119

Chapter 12: Incendiary Attack ······················ 143

Chapter 13: Using Spies ······························ 151

孙子兵法

SUN-TZU: THE ART OF WARFARE

计第一

计,《说文》:"会也,筭也。"这里指篇末所说的"庙筭"。筭,是一种原始计数工具,与筹、策是同类性质的东西。古代出兵之前先要在庙堂上用这种工具计算敌我优劣,叫做"庙筭"。庙筭是出兵之前的决策,先于野战和攻城。古人认为,一国君将必先操握胜算,然后才能出兵,这是兵略的第一要义。所以《汉书·艺文志·兵书略》分兵书为四类,其中"兵权谋类"即以"先计而后战"为基本特征。

Chapter 1:
On Assessments

计第一

1. 孙子曰：

   兵者，国之大事。死生之地，存亡之道，不可不察也。

   孙子说：军事，是国家的大事。地形的死生之势（死
   地、生地），战场上的存亡胜败，不可不加以了解。

2. 故经之以五事，校之以计，而索其情：一曰道，二曰天，三
   曰地，四曰将，五曰法。

   所以凭下述五项衡量，通过计算，加以核实，弄清情
   况：一是道义，二是天时，三是地利，四是将领，五是法规。

   道者，令民与上同意，可与之死，可与之生，而不（畏）
   危也；

   道义，是指使人民与国君同心同德，可以和国君一起
   死，一起生，而绝不违背；

   天者，阴阳、寒暑、时制也；

   天时，是指阴阳向背、天气冷暖和四时变换；

   地者，远近、险易、广狭、死生也；

   地利，是指地形的远近、险夷、宽窄、死生；

Chapter 1: On Assessments

1. Master Sun said:

    War is a vital matter of state. It is the field on which life or death is determined and the road that leads to either survival or ruin, and must be examined with the greatest care.

2. Therefore, to gauge the outcome of war we must appraise the situation on the basis of the following five criteria, and compare the two sides by assessing their relative strengths. The first of the five criteria is the way (*tao*), the second is climate, the third is terrain, the fourth is command, and the fifth is regulation.

    The way (*tao*) is what brings the thinking of the people in line with their superiors. Hence, you can send them to their deaths or let them live, and they will have no misgivings one way or the other.

    Climate is light and shadow, heat and cold, and the rotation of the seasons.

    Terrain refers to the fall of the land, proximate distances, difficulty of passage, the degree of openness, and the viability of

计第一

将者，智、信、仁、勇、严也；

将领，是指指挥者的智慧、诚信、仁慈、勇敢、严明；

法者，曲制、官道、主用也。

法规，是指队形编制、官吏委派、财务管理。

凡此五者，将莫不闻，知之者胜，不知者不胜。

凡此五项，身为将领，不可不加过问，知道的就能胜利，不知道的就不能胜利。

故校之以计，而索其情，曰：

所以通过计算，加以核实，弄清情况，就要问：

主孰有道？将孰有能？天地孰得？法令孰行？兵众孰强？士卒孰练？赏罚孰明？吾以此知胜负矣。

国君哪一方有道义？将领哪一方有才能？天时地利哪一方能掌握？法规号令哪一方能执行？军队哪一方更强大？士兵哪一方更精锐？赏罚哪一方更严明？我凭这些就能判断胜负。

Chapter 1 : On Assessments

the land for deploying troops.

Command is a matter of wisdom, integrity, humanity, courage, and discipline.

And regulation entails organizational effectiveness, a chain of command, and a structure for logistical support.

All commanders are familiar with these five criteria, yet it is he who masters them who takes the victory, while he who does not will not prevail.

Therefore, to gauge the outcome of war we must compare the two sides by assessing their relative strengths. This is to ask the following questions:

Which ruler has the way (*tao*)?

Which commander has the greater ability?

Which side has the advantages of climate and terrain?

Which army follows regulations and obeys orders more strictly?

Which army has superior strength?

Whose officers and men are better trained?

Which side is more strict and impartial in meting out rewards and punishments?

计第一

将听吾计，用之必胜，留之；将不听吾计，用之必败，去之。

如果〔受计者〕服从我的计谋，使用必将获胜，就留用他；如果〔受计者〕不服从我的计谋，使用必将失败，就撤掉他。

3. 计利以听，乃为之势，以佐其外。势者，因利而制权也。

计谋有利并得到执行，才去制造"势"，用来辅助出兵国外后的行动。"势"，就是利用优势，制造机变。

兵者，诡道也。故能而示之不能，用而示之不用，近而示之远，远而示之近。利而诱之，乱而取之，实而备之，强而避之，怒而挠之，卑而骄之，佚而劳之，亲而离之。攻其无备，出其不意。此兵家之胜，不可先传也。

军事，是诡诈之道。所以能反而示以不能，用反而示以不用，近反而示以远，远反而示以近。敌贪利就诱惑它，敌混乱就袭击它，敌充实就防备它，敌强大就躲避它，敌恼怒就骚扰它，敌卑怯就使之骄傲，敌安逸就使之劳累，敌亲密

Chapter 1: On Assessments

On the basis of this comparison I know who will win and who will lose.

If you heed my assessments, dispatching troops into battle would mean certain victory, and I will stay. If you do not heed them, dispatching troops would mean certain defeat, and I will leave.

3. Having heard what can be gained from my assessments, shape a strategic advantage (*shih*) from them to strengthen our position. By "strategic advantage" I mean making the most of favorable conditions (*yin*) and tilting the scales in our favor.

Warfare is the art (*tao*) of deceit. Therefore, when able, seem to be unable; when ready, seem unready; when nearby, seem far away; and when far away, seem near. If the enemy seeks some advantage, entice him with it. If he is in disorder, attack him and take him. If he is formidable, prepare against him. If he is strong, evade him. If he is incensed, provoke him. If he is humble, encourage his arrogance. If he is rested, wear him down. If he is internally harmonious, sow divisiveness in his ranks. Attack where he is not prepared; go by way of places

就使之离心。进攻其毫无防备之处，出击其意想不到之地。
这就是兵家得胜的诀窍，不可能事先传授。

4. 夫未战而庙算胜者，得算多也；未战而庙算不胜者，得算少
也。多算胜少算（不胜），而况于无算乎！吾以此观之，胜负
见矣。

　　凡是没有出兵交战就在"庙算"上先已获胜，是由于得
到的"算"较多；没有出兵交战就在"庙算"上先已失败，
是由于得到的"算"较少。得到"算"多的胜过得到"算"
少的，更何况是那没有得到"算"的呢！我凭这些去看，胜
负之分就一清二楚了。

where it would never occur to him you would go. These are the military strategist's calculations for victory – they cannot be settled in advance.

4. It is by scoring many points that one wins the war beforehand in the temple rehearsal of the battle; it is by scoring few points that one loses the war beforehand in the temple rehearsal of the battle. The side that scores many points will win; the side that scores few points will not win, let alone the side that scores no points at all. When I examine it in this way, the outcome of the war becomes apparent.

作战第二

　　本篇是讲庙算之后的兴师用兵，即"先计而后战"的"而后战"。这里"作"是兴、起之义，"战"指出兵以后的野战。

　　"战"字有广狭含义的不同。广义的"战"是泛指一切实战，狭义的"战"则区别于攻城，专指野战。古代实行国野制度，国是王或诸侯宗庙所在的城邑，野是环绕这种城邑的乡村。野多为平衍之地，两国交兵于野，叫做野战，往往经过野战才发展为攻城。

　　在本篇中，作者指出当时战争动员规模庞大，深入敌国，远离后方，难以补充给养装备。如果野战不利，相持过久，必将导致国弊民穷。因此，把速决和就地补充给养装备（夺取敌方）奉为野战的基本原则。

Chapter 2:
On Waging Battle

作战第二

1. 孙子曰：

凡用兵之法，驰车千驷，革车千乘，带甲十万，千里馈粮。〔则〕内外之费，宾客之用，胶漆之材，车甲之奉，日费千金，然后十万之师举矣。

孙子说：

一般的用兵规模，需要驰车一千辆，革车一千辆，披带铠甲的战士十万人，千里迢迢运送粮食。这样国内外的各种费用开支，包括招待宾客、采办胶与漆等材料、供应车马兵甲，每天要花费千金之巨，然后这支十万大军才能开拔。

2. 其用战也，胜久则钝兵挫锐，攻城则力屈。久暴师则国用不足。夫钝兵挫锐，屈力殚货，则诸侯乘其弊而起，虽有智者，不能善其后矣。

如果作战是靠持久而取胜，那么就会消耗兵力，挫伤锐气，攻城就会感到力量不足。如果长期把军队暴露在国外，那么国家财政就会感到拮据。而消耗兵力，挫伤锐气，人力、财源耗尽，那么诸侯各国就会乘此危机举兵来袭，即使足智多谋的人，也不能收拾残局。

Chapter 2: On Waging Battle

1. Master Sun said:

   The art of warfare is this:

   For an army of one thousand fast four–horse chariots, one thousand four–horse leather–covered wagons, and one hundred thousand armor–clad troops, and for the provisioning of this army over a distance of a thousand *li*, what with expenses at home and on the field, including foreign envoys and advisors, materials such as glue and lacquer, and the maintenance of chariots and armor, only when you have in hand one thousand pieces of gold for each day can the hundred thousand troops be mobilized.

2. In joining battle, seek the quick victory. If battle is protracted, your weapons will be blunted and your troops demoralized. If you lay siege to a walled city, you exhaust your strength. If your armies are kept in the field for a long time, your national reserves will not suffice. Where you have blunted your weapons, demoralized your troops, exhausted your strength and depleted all available resources, the neighboring rulers will take advantage of your adversity to strike. And even with the wisest of counsel, you will not be able to turn the ensuing consequences to the good.

作战第二

故兵闻拙速，未睹巧之久也。夫兵久而国利者，未之有也。

所以军事上只听说过简单的速决，没有见过巧妙的持久。用兵持久而对国家有利，是从来没有的。

3. 故不尽知用兵之害者，则不能尽知用兵之利也。

所以不完全懂得用兵的害处，就不能完全懂得用兵的利处。

善用兵者，役不再籍，粮不三载，取用于国，因粮于敌，故军食可足也。

善于用兵的人，丘役不多次征发，粮食也不多次输送，先从国内征粮，再从敌方得到补充，所以军需用粮可以满足。

国之贫于师者远输，远输则百姓贫；近师者贵卖，贵卖则百姓财竭；财竭则急于丘役。（力屈）〔屈力〕（财殚）中原，内虚于家，百姓之费，十去其（七）〔六〕；公家之费，破车罢马，甲胄矢弓，戟楯矛橹，丘牛大车，十去其（六）〔七〕。

国家由于军队而造成贫困，主要在于长途运输，长途运输百姓就会贫困；靠近军队驻地往往物价腾贵，物价腾贵百姓就会财源枯竭；百姓财源断绝，就会给丘役的征发造成压力。人力耗尽于原野之上，家家内部空虚，百姓的花费，十

Chapter 2: On Waging Battle

Thus in war, I have heard tell of a foolish haste, but I have yet to see a case of cleverly dragging on the hostilities. There has never been a state that has benefited from an extended war.

3. Hence, if one is not fully cognizant of the evils of waging war, he cannot be fully cognizant either of how to turn it to best account.

The expert in using the military does not conscript soldiers more than once or transport his provisions repeatedly from home. He carries his military equipment with him, and commandeers (*yin*) his provisions from the enemy. Thus he has what he needs to feed his army.

A state is impoverished by its armies when it has to supply them at a great distance. To supply an army at a great distance is to impoverish one's people. On the other hand, in the vicinity of the armies, the price of goods goes up. Where goods are expensive, you exhaust your resources, and once you have exhausted your resources, you will be forced to increase district exactions for the military. All your strength is spent on the battlefield, and the families on the home front are left destitute.

作战第二

分丧失掉六分；公家的花费，包括车、马的损耗，以及铠甲、头盔、弓矢、矛戟和盾牌，还有丘牛和丘牛所驾的辎重车，十分丧失掉七分。

故智将务食于敌，食敌一钟，当吾二十钟；秆一石，当吾二十石。

所以聪明的将领务求取食于敌，吃敌人一钟，等于自己的二十钟；豆秸、禾秆一石，等于自己的二十石。

故杀敌者，怒也；取敌之利者，货也。车战，得车十乘以上，赏其先得者而更其旌旗。车杂而乘之，卒善而养之，是谓胜敌而益强。

所以杀敌是靠激发士兵对敌人的仇恨，夺取敌人是靠用财货奖赏士兵。车战中若缴获战车十辆以上，要奖赏最先获得者并更换车上的旗帜，将缴获的战车混杂使用，俘虏的士兵善加供养，这就叫战胜敌人而自己也更强大。

Chapter 2: On Waging Battle

The toll to the people will have been some 70 percent of their property; the toll to the public coffers in terms of broken–down chariots and worn–out horses, body armor and helmets, cross-bows and bolts, halberds and bucklers, lances and shields, draft oxen and heavy supply wagons will be some 60 percent of its reserves.

Therefore, the wise commander does his best to feed his army from enemy soil. To consume one measure of the enemy's provisions is equal to twenty of our own; to use up one bale of the enemy's fodder is equal to twenty of our own.

Killing the enemy is a matter of arousing the anger of our men; snatching the enemy's wealth is a matter of dispensing the spoils. Thus, in a chariot battle here more than ten war chariots have been captured, reward those who captured the first one and replace the enemy's flags and standards with our own. Mix the chariots in with our ranks and send them back into battle; provide for the captured soldiers and treat them well. This is called increasing our own strength in the process of defeating the army.

作战第二

4. 故兵贵胜，不贵久。

   所以军事上只重取胜，而不重持久。

5. 故知兵之将，民之司命，国家安危之主也。

   所以真正懂得军事的将领是人民生死和国家安危的主宰。

Chapter 2: On Waging Battle

4. Hence, in war prize the quick victory, not the protracted engagement.

5. Thus, the commander who understands war is the final arbiter of people's lives, and lord over the security of the state.

谋攻第三

本篇是讲庙算、野战之后的攻城。"谋攻"是指用智谋攻城，即不是专恃武力强攻，而是用打乱敌人的部署、沮丧敌人的意志造成形格势禁，迫使守敌投降。

在攻坚手段极为有限的古代，攻城往往徒然费时折兵，这是作者之所以特别重视以谋攻城的直接原因（正像上篇所言速决是针对当时战役旷日持久而发一样）。但作者在论述这种以谋攻城的方法时，却并不停留于现象本身，而是把它提高到战略学的高度来认识。他从战争的目的是最大限度地消灭敌人和保存自己这一点出发，提出一种"全利"的原则，聪明地看出，战争从"伐谋"到"伐交"到"伐兵"到"攻城"，这一逐步升级的过程，可能预示着一种逆过程，即"伐谋"的重新出现。并且作者还论述了力量对比与攻守形势的关系。

Chapter 3:
Planning the Attack

谋攻第三

1. 孙子曰：

   夫用兵之法，全国为上，破国次之；全军为上，破军次之；全旅为上，破旅次之；全卒为上，破卒次之；全伍为上，破伍次之。

   孙子说：

   用兵之法，以完整地战胜一个"国"为上，击破后战胜一个"国"次之；完整地战胜一个"军"为上，击破后战胜一个"军"次之；完整地战胜一个"旅"为上，击破后战胜一个"旅"次之；完整地战胜一个"卒"为上，击破后战胜一个"卒"次之；完整地战胜一个"伍"为上，击破后战胜一个"伍"次之。

2. 是故百战百胜，非善之善者也；不战而屈人之兵，善之善者也。

   所以百战百胜，算不上真正的高明；不战而使敌军屈服，才算得上真正的高明。

   故上兵伐谋，其次伐交，其次伐兵，其下攻城。

   所以军事手段以智谋战为上，其次为外交战，其次为野战，而以攻城为最下。

   攻城之法，为不得已。修橹轒辒，具器械，三月而后成；距堙，又三月而后已。将不胜其忿而蚁附之，杀士卒三

Chapter 3: Planning the Attack

1. Master Sun said:

    The art of warfare is this:

    It is best to keep one's own state intact; to crush the enemy's state is only a second best. It is best to keep one's own army, battalion, company, or five-man squad intact; to crush the enemy's army, battalion, company, or five-man squad is only a second best.

2. So to win a hundred victories in a hundred battles is not the highest excellence; the highest excellence is to subdue the enemy's army without fighting at all.

    Therefore, the best military policy is to attack strategies; the next to attack alliances; the next to attack soldiers; and the worst to assault walled cities.

    Resort to assaulting walled cities only when there is no other choice. To construct siege screens and armored personnel vehi-

谋攻第三

分之一，而城不拔者，此攻之灾也。

攻城的办法，是出于不得已。修造"橹"（带望楼的战车）和"辒"（有皮甲装护的四轮攻城车），准备各种器具，要三个月才能完成；"距堙"（攻城用的土山），又要三个月才能完成。将领怒不可遏，而命士兵"蚁附"（像蚂蚁一样缘墙而上）攻城，导致三分之一的士卒白白送命，而城却仍然攻不下来，这是攻城的灾难。

故善用兵者，屈人之兵而非战也，拔人之城而非攻也，毁人之国而非久也，必以全争于天下，故兵不顿而利可全，此谋攻之法也。

所以善用兵的人，使敌军屈服不是靠野战，拔取敌人的城邑不是靠强攻，毁灭敌人的国家不是靠持久，一定要本着"完整取胜"的原则来与天下各国竞争，所以既不用消耗兵力而又能保全利益，这就是用智谋攻城的方法。

3. 故用兵之法，十则围之，五则攻之，倍则分之，敌则能战之，少则能逃之，不若则能避之。故小敌之坚，大敌之擒也。

所以用兵之法，十倍于敌就围歼它，五倍于敌就进攻它，两倍于敌就分割它，势均力敌要能列阵而战，略弱于敌要能组织退却，敌我悬殊要能避免接触。所以小的对手若能

Chapter 3: Planning the Attack

cles and to assemble all of the military equipment and weaponry necessary will take three months, and to amass earthen mounds against the walls will take another three months. And if your commander, unable to control his temper, sends your troops swarming at the walls, your casualties will be one in three and still you will not have taken the city. This is the kind of calamity that befalls you in laying siege.

Therefore, the expert in using the military subdues the enemy's forces without going to battle, takes the enemy's walled cities without launching an attack, and crushes the enemy's state without a protracted war. He must use the principle of keeping himself intact to compete in the world. Thus, his weapons will not be blunted and he can keep his edge intact. This then is the art of planning the attack.

3. Therefore the art of using troops is this:

When ten times the enemy strength, surround him; when five times, attack him; when double, engage him; when you and the enemy are equally matched, be able to divide him; when you are inferior in numbers, be able to take the defensive; and when

集中力量，大的对手也会为之所擒。

4. 夫将者，国之辅也。辅周则国必强，辅隙则国必弱。

　　将领，是国家的辅佐。辅佐周详则国家一定强大，辅佐疏忽则国家一定衰弱。

　　故君之所以患于军者三：不知军之不可以进而谓之进，不知军之不可以退而谓之退，是谓縻军；不知三军之事而同三军之政，则军士惑矣；不知三军之权而同三军之任，则军士疑矣。

　　所以国君给军队造成危害有三种情况：不知军队不可以进攻而硬要它进攻，不知军队不可以退却而硬要它退却，这就叫牵制军队；不知三军的事务而硬要参与三军之事的管理，士兵就会迷惑；不知三军的权限而硬要参与三军之职的委任，士兵就会怀疑。

　　三军既惑且疑，则诸侯之难至矣。是谓乱军引胜。

　　三军将士既迷惑又怀疑，那么诸侯各国举兵来袭的灾难就会降临。这就叫扰乱自己的军队而导致敌人的胜利。

Chapter 3: Planning the Attack

you are no match for the enemy, be able to avoid him. Thus what serves as secure defense against a small army will only be captured by a large one.

4. The commander is the side–guard on the carriage of state. When this guard is in place, the state will certainly be strong; where it is defective, the state will certainly be weak.

There are three ways in which the ruler can bring grief to his army:

To order an advance, not realizing the army is in no position to do so, or do order a retreat, not realizing the army is in no position to withdraw – this is called "hobbling the army."

To interfere in the administration of the army while being ignorant of its internal affairs will confuse officers and soldiers alike.

To interfere in military assignments while being ignorant of exigencies will lose him the confidence of his men.

Once his army has become confused and he has lost the confidence of his men, aggression from his neighboring rulers will be upon him. This is called sowing disorder in your own ranks and throwing away the victory.

谋攻第三

5. 故知胜有五：知可以（与战）〔战与〕不可以（与）战者胜，识众寡之用者胜，上下同欲者胜，以虞待不虞者胜，将能而君不御者胜。此五者，知胜之道也。

　　所以判断胜利有五条：知道自己可以作战或不可以作战的一方胜利；懂得力量配置的一方胜利；上下同心同德的一方胜利；以有准备对付无准备的一方胜利；将领有才干而国君不加干预的一方胜利。这五条，是判断胜利的根本。

　　故曰：知彼知己，百战不殆；不知彼而知己，一胜一负；不知彼，不知己，每战必败。

　　所以说：了解对手也了解自己，才能常胜不败；不了解对手而只了解自己，就会有胜有负；既不了解对手，也不了解自己，就会每战必败。

Chapter 3: Planning the Attack

5. Therefore there are five factors in anticipating which side will win:

    The side that knows when to fight and when not to will take the victory.

    The side that understands how to deal with numerical superiority and inferiority in the deployment of troops will take the victory.

    The side that has superiors and subordinates united in purpose will take the victory.

    The side that fields a fully prepared army against one that is not will take the victory.

    The side on which the commander is able and the ruler does not interfere will take the victory.

    These five factors are the way (*tao*) of anticipating victory.

    Thus it is said:

    He who knows the enemy and himself

    Will never in a hundred battles be at risk;

    He who does not know the enemy but knows himself

    Will sometimes win and sometimes lose;

    He who knows neither the enemy nor himself

    Will be at risk in every battle.

形第四

　　"形"与下篇所论"势"是一对矛盾概念，也合称为"形势"。《汉书·艺文志·兵书略》载任宏论次兵书为四种，第一种是"权谋"，第二种就是"形势"，而所谓"权谋"也包括"形势"在内。任宏所说的"权谋"，应属战略学的范畴，特征是"以正守国，以奇用兵，先计而后战，兼形势，包阴阳，用技巧者也"。而"形势"应属战术学的范畴，特征是"雷动风举，后发而先至，离合背向，变化无常，以轻疾制敌者也"。在《孙子》书中，"形"含有形象、形体等义，是指战争中客观、有常、易见的诸因素。它主要同实力的概念、优势的概念有关。

Chapter 4:
Strategic Positions
(Hsing)

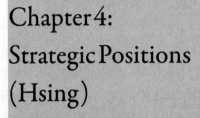

形第四

1. 孙子曰：

　　昔之善战者，先为不可胜，以待敌之可胜。不可胜在己，可胜在敌。故善战者，能为不可胜，不能使敌之必可胜。故曰：胜可知，而不可为。不可胜者，守也；可胜者，攻也。守则不足，攻则有余。善守者藏于九地之下，善攻者动于九天之上，故能自保而全胜也。

　　孙子说：

　　从前善战的人，总是先造成自己不可战胜，然后等待敌人可以被战胜。不可战胜在于自己，可以战胜在于敌人。所以善战的人，能够造成自己不可战胜，却不能使敌人必定被战胜。所以说：胜利可以预知，而不可强为。不可胜的一方，取守势；可以胜的一方，取攻势。取守势是因为力量不足，取攻势是因为力量有余。善于防守的人，好比隐伏藏匿在深不可测的地底；善于进攻的人，好比突然降临自高不可及的天空，所以能保存自己的力量，同时完整地夺取胜利。

2. 见胜不过众人之所知，非善之善者也；战胜而天下曰善，非善之善者也。故举秋毫不为多力，见日月不为明目，闻雷霆不为聪耳。古之所谓善战者，胜于易胜者也。故善战者之胜

Chapter 4: Strategic Positions

1. Master Sun said:

   Of old the expert in battle would first make himself invincible and then wait for the enemy to expose his vulnerability. Invincibility depends on oneself; vulnerability lies with the enemy. Therefore the expert in battle can make himself invincible, but cannot guarantee for certain the vulnerability of the enemy. Hence it is said:

   > Victory can be anticipated,
   >
   > But it cannot be forced.

   Being invincible lies with defense; the vulnerability of the enemy comes with the attack. If one assumes a defensive posture, it is because the enemy's strength is overwhelming; if one launches the attack, it is because the enemy's strength is deficient. The expert at defense conceals himself in the deepest recesses of the earth; the expert on the attack strikes from out of the highest reaches of the heavens. Thus he is able to both protect himself and to take the complete victory.

2. To anticipate the victory is not going beyond the understanding of the common run; it is not the highest excellence. To win in battle so that the whole world says "Excellent!" is not the high-

也，无智名，无勇功，故其战胜不忒。不忒者，其所措胜，胜已败者也。

预见胜利不出众人所知，算不上高明；战胜而天下誉为高明，也算不上高明。所以举起秋毫算不上力大，看见日月算不上眼明，听见雷霆算不上耳聪。古代所谓善战的人，是取胜于容易被战胜的对手。所以善战的人取胜，没有智慧之名，没有勇武之功，以至稳操胜券而没有差错。没有差错，是因为他的举措本身就是有胜利把握的，已经取胜于注定失败的敌人。

故善战者，立于不败之地，而不失敌之败也。是故胜兵先胜而后求战，败兵先战而后求胜。

所以善战的人，总是立于不败之地，而又不失去能造成敌人失败的机会。所以能够取胜的军队总是先有胜利的把握然后才去求战，必将失败的军队总是先投入战斗然后才想侥幸而取胜。

善用兵者，修道而保法，故能为胜败之政。

善于用兵的人，修明政治并遵循法度，所以能掌握胜败。

est excellence. Hence, to life an autumn hair is no mark of strength; to see the sun and moon is no mark of clear–sightedness; to hear a thunder clap is no mark of keen hearing. He whom the ancients called an expert in battle gained victory where victory was easily gained. Thus the battle of the expert is never an exceptional victory, nor does it win him reputation for wisdom or credit for courage. His victories in battle are unerring. Unerring means that he acts where victory is certain, and conquers an enemy that has already lost.

Therefore, the expert in battle takes his stand on ground that is unassailable, and does not miss his chance to defeat the enemy. For this reason, the victorious army only enters battle after having first won the victory, while the defeated army only seeks victory after having first entered the fray.

The expert in using the military builds upon the way (*tao*) and holds fast to military regulations, and thus is able to be the arbiter of victory and defeat.

形第四

3. 兵法：一曰度，二曰量，三曰数，四曰称，五曰胜。地生度，度生量，量生数，数生称，称生胜。故胜兵若以镒称铢，败兵若以铢称镒。

出军之法包含了五个环节：一是丈度，二是称量，三是人数，四是比较，五是胜利。土地产生土地面积的丈度；土地面积的丈度决定粮食产量的称量；粮食产量的称量决定可养农户和出兵的人数；可养农户和出兵的人数决定敌我力量的对比；敌我力量的对比决定胜负。所以胜利的军队好比是用镒来称量铢，失败的军队好比是用铢来称量镒。

4. 胜者之战〔民也〕，若决积水于千仞之溪者，形也。

在实力对比上取得优势的一方，使用人民作战，就像从千仞之高的溪谷往下放积水，这就是"形"啊。

Chapter 4: Strategic Positions

3. Factors in the art of warfare are: First, calculations; second, quantities; third logistics; fourth, the balance of power; and fifth, the possibility of victory. Calculations are based on the terrain, estimates of available quantities of goods are based these calculations, logistical strength is based on estimates of available quantities of goods, the balance of power is based on logistical strength, and the possibility of victory is based on the balance of power.

4. Thus a victorious army is like weighing in a full hundredweight against a few ounces, and a defeated army is like pitting a few ounces against a hundredweight. It is a matter of strategic positioning (*hsing*) that the army that has this weight of victory on its side, in launching its men into battle, can be likened to the cascading of pent−up waters thundering through a steep gorge.

势第五

"势"含有态势之义，是指战争中人为、易变、潜在的诸因素。它与"形"相反，多指随机的和能动的东西，如指挥的灵活、士气的勇怯，等等。在《计》中，作者把"势"看作是利用优势，制造机变（"势者，因利而制权也"）。在本篇中，作者则强调指出，"势"是以"奇正"之术（兵力的战术配置）为主要内容，并且在实施中要取决于士兵临战的实际发挥，特别是随环境变化的"勇怯"（"勇怯，势也"）。

战国时期，由于整个战争方式和军事制度的改变，军事艺术也相应发生变化。战国时期的军队是以"隆势诈，尚功利"为特点（见《荀子·议兵》）。当时的许多大军事家，如孙膑即以"贵势"而著称（见《吕氏春秋·不二》）。出土简本《孙子兵法》，其篇次也是以《势》在前而《形》在后。

Chapter 5:
Strategic Advantage
(Shih)

势第五

1. 孙子曰：

   凡治众如治寡，分数是也；斗众如斗寡，形名是也；三
军之众，可使（必）〔毕〕受敌而无败者，奇正是也；兵之所
加，如以碫投卵者，虚实是也。

   孙子说：

   管理大量士兵如同管理少量士兵，是靠"分数"；指挥大
量士兵作战如同指挥少量士兵作战，是靠"形名"；三军士
兵，可使四面受敌也不会失败，是靠"奇正"；兵力所向，如
同以石击卵，是靠"虚实"。

2. 凡战者，以正合，以奇胜。故善出奇者，无穷如天地，不竭
如江海。终而复始，日月是也；死而更生，四时是也。

   一般作战，是以"正"兵接敌，以"奇"兵取胜。所以
善用"奇"兵出击的人，〔其战术变化〕无穷有如天地，不竭
有如江海。结束了又重新开始，那是日月出没；死去了又重
新复活，那是四季变换。

   声不过五，五声之变，不可胜听也；色不过五，五色之
变，不可胜观也；味不过五，五味之变，不可胜尝也；战势
不过奇正，奇正之变，不可胜穷也。奇正相生，如循环之无

Chapter 5: Strategic Advantage

1. Master Sun said:

   In general, it is organization that makes managing many soldiers the same as managing a few. It is communication with flags and pennants that makes fighting with many soldiers the same as fighting with a few. It is "surprise" (*ch'i*) and "straightforward" (*cheng*) operations that enable one's army to withstand the full assault of the enemy force and remain undefeated. It is the distinction between "weak points" and "strong points" that makes one's army falling upon the enemy a whetstone being hurled at eggs.

2. Generally in battle use the "straightforward" to engage the enemy and the "surprise" to win the victory. Thus the expert at delivering the surprise assault is as boundless as the heavens and earth, and as inexhaustible as the rivers and seas. Like the sun and moon, he sets only to rise again; like the four seasons, he passes only to return again.

   There are no more than five cardinal notes, yet in combination, they produce more sounds than could possibly be heard; there are no more than five cardinal colors, yet in combination,

端，孰能穷之哉！

音阶不过五种，五种音阶的变化，听也听不过来；颜色不过五种，五种颜色的变化，看也看不过来；味道不过五种，五种味道的变化，尝也尝不过来；作战的态势不过"奇正"，但"奇正"的变化，是不可穷尽的。"奇"与"正"相互转化，如同圆圈找不到终端，谁能够穷尽它呢！

3. **激水之疾，至于漂石者，势也；鸷鸟之疾，至于毁折者，节也。故善战者，其势险，其节短。势如彍弩，节如发机。**

湍激的流水速度之快，竟使水中的石头漂起，是借助水势；猛禽的搏击，竟使小动物当即毙命，是靠掌握节奏。所以善战的人，他所造成的态势是险峻的，他所掌握的节奏是短促的。制造态势有如张满强弩，掌握节奏有如扣动扳机。

4. **纷纷纭纭，斗乱而不可乱；浑浑沌沌，形圆而不可败。**

纷纷纭纭，战斗混乱却有条不紊；混混沌沌，阵容严整而无隙可乘。

Chapter 5: Strategic Advantage

they produce more shades and hues than could possibly be seen; there are no more than five cardinal tastes, yet in combination, they produce more flavors than could possibly be tasted. For gaining strategic advantage (*shih*) in battle, there are no more than "surprise" and "straightforward" operations, ye tin combination, they produce inexhaustible possibilities. "Surprise" and "straightforward" operations give rise to each other endlessly just as a ring is without a beginning or an end. And who can exhaust their possibilities?

3. That the velocity of cascading water can send boulders bobbing about is due to its strategic advantage (*shih*). That a bird of prey when it strikes can smash its victims to pieces is due to its timing. So it is with the expert at battle that his strategic advantage (*shih*) is channeled and his timing is precise. His strategic advantage (*shih*) is like a drawn crossbow and his timing is like releasing the trigger.

4. Even amidst the tumult and the clamor of battle, in all its confusion, he cannot be confused. Even amidst the melee and the brawl of battle, with positions shifting every which way, he can-

势第五

乱生于治，怯生于勇，弱生于强。治乱，数也。勇怯，势也。强弱，形也。

混乱产生于整齐，怯懦产生于勇敢，虚弱产生于强大。整齐与混乱，属于"分数"；勇敢与怯懦，属于"势"；强大与虚弱，属于"形"。

5. 故善动敌者，形之，敌必从之；予之，敌必取之。以利动之，以（本）〔卒〕待之。

所以善于调动敌人的将帅做出样子，敌必信从；给予好处，敌必接受。用小利去调动敌人，用重兵去守候敌人。

故善战者，求之于势，不责于人，故能择人而任势。任势者，其战人也，如转木石。木石之性，安则静，危则动，方则止，圆则行。

所以善战的人，只求之于"势"，而不求之于人，所以能放弃人而依赖"势"。依赖"势"的人，指挥士兵作战，有如转动滚木圆石。木头石块的特性，平放则静止，倾侧则滚动，方形则停止，圆形则前进。

not be defeated.

Disorder is born from order; cowardice from courage; weakness from strength. The line between disorder and order lies in logistics (*shu*); between cowardice and courage, in strategic advantage (*shih*); and between weakness and strength, in strategic positioning (*hsing*).

5. Thus the expert at getting the enemy to make his move shows himself (*hsing*), and the enemy is certain to follow. He baits the enemy, and the enemy is certain to take it. In so doing, he moves the enemy, and lies in wait for him with his full force.

The expert at battle seeks his victory from strategic advantage (*shih*) and does not demand it from his men. He is thus able to select the right men and exploit the strategic advantage (*shih*). He who exploits the strategic advantage (*shih*) sends his men into battle like rolling logs and boulders. It is the nature of logs and boulders that on flat ground, they are stationary, but on steep ground, they roll; the square in shape tends to stop but the round tends to roll.

势第五

6. 故善战人之势，如转圆石于千仞之山者，势也。

所以善于指挥士兵作战的人所造成的"势"，有如从千仞高山上滚下圆石，这就是"势"啊！

Chapter 5: Strategic Advantage

6. Thus, that the strategic advantage (*shih*) of the expert commander in exploiting his men in battle can be likened to rolling round boulders down a steep ravine thousands of feet high says something about his strategic advantage (*shih*).

虚实第六

简本"虚实"作"实虚"。"虚实"是指兵力的相对集中和相对分散。它与"奇正"不同,"奇正"是将己方兵力投入实际战斗时所做的战术配置,而"虚实"则是指通过分散集结的运动变化以造成预定会战地点上的我强敌劣("我专而敌分"、"我众敌寡")。作者也把这种"避实击虚"、"以众击寡"的运用之妙称作"形兵"。这种"形兵"的"形"是一种人为造成的态势,具有相当大的随机性质,所以作者也称之为"无形"。

Chapter 6:
Weak Points and Strong
Points

虚实第六

1. 孙子曰：

   凡先处战地而待敌者佚，后处战地而趋战者劳。故善战者，致人而不致于人。能使敌人自至者，利之也；能使敌人不得至者，害之也。故敌佚能劳之，饱能饥之，安能动之，出其所（不）〔必〕趋，趋其所不意。

   孙子说：

   一般先到达会战地点等待敌人的则安逸，后到达会战地点仓卒应战的则疲劳。所以善战的人，总是使敌人前来就我而不是自己前往就敌。能使敌人自动前来，是以利引诱的结果；能使敌人不能前来，是以害阻挠的结果。所以敌人安逸能使之疲劳，饱食能使之饥饿，安静能使之骚动，向敌人必定前往的方向出动，却使敌人意料不到我军正在前往。

2. 行千里而不劳者，行于无人之地也；攻而必取者，攻其所不守也；守而必固者，守其所（不）〔必〕攻也。故善攻者，敌不知其所守；善守者，敌不知其所攻。

   千里行军而不觉疲劳，是由于行进在没有敌人的地方；攻打而一定夺取，是由于攻打的是敌人未经设防之处；防守而一定牢固，是由于设防于敌人必然进攻之处。所以善于进攻的人，敌人不知该在哪里设防；善于防守的人，敌人不知该从哪里进攻。

Chapter 6: Weak Points and Strong Points

1. Master Sun said:

   Generally he who first occupies the field of battle to await the enemy will be rested; he who comes later and hastens into battle will be weary. Thus the expert in battle moves the enemy, and is not moved by him. Getting the enemy to come of his own accord is a matter of making things easy for him; stopping him from coming is a matter of obstructing him. Thus being able to wear down a well–rested enemy, to starve one that is well–provisioned, and to move one that is settled, lies in going by way of places where the enemy must hasten in defense.

2. To march a thousand *li* without becoming weary is because one marches through territory where there is no enemy presence. To attack with the confidence of taking one's objective is because one attacks what the enemy does not defend. To defend with the confidence of keeping one's charge secure is because one defends where the enemy will not attack. Thus against the expert in the attack, the enemy does not know where to defend, and against the expert in defense, the enemy does not know

虚实第六

微乎微乎，至于无形；神乎神乎，至于无声，故能为敌之司命。

微妙啊微妙，竟然无形可见；神秘啊神秘，竟然无声可闻，所以可以做敌人命运的主宰。

进而不可御者，冲其虚也；退而不可追者，(速)〔远〕而不可及也。

前进而不可抵御，是由于冲击敌人的薄弱之处；撤退而不可追击，是由于远远甩开敌人让它赶不上。

故我欲战，敌虽高垒深沟，不得不与我战者，攻其所必救也；我不欲战，虽画地而守之，敌不得与我战者，乖其所之也。

所以我要决战，敌人哪怕有高垒深沟，也不得不与我决战，这是由于攻它必须援救之处；我不愿意决战，哪怕是划地为营而据守，敌人却不能与我决战，这是由于反其意而行之。

故形人而我无形，则我专而敌分。我专为一，敌分为十，是以十攻其一也，则我众敌寡。能以众击寡，则吾之所

Chapter 6: Weak Points and Strong Points

where to strike.

> So veiled and subtle,
>
> To the point of having no form (*hsing*);
>
> So mysterious and miraculous,
>
> To the point of making no sound.
>
> Therefore he can be arbiter of the enemy's fate.

In advancing he cannot be resisted because he bursts through the enemy's weak points; in withdrawing he cannot be pursued because, being so quick, he cannot be caught.

Thus, if we want to fight, the enemy has no choice but to engage us, even though safe behind his high walls and deep moats, because we strike at what he must rescue. If we do not want to fight, the enemy cannot engage us, even though we have no more around us than a drawn line, because we divert him to a different objective.

If we can make the enemy show his position (*hsing*) while concealing ours from him, we will be at full force where he is di-

虚实第六

与战者约矣。

所以我能驱策敌人而不被敌人驱策，以致造成我方的兵力集中和敌方的兵力分散。我将兵力集中为一股，敌人将兵力分散为十股，便相当于我以十倍于敌的兵力攻击敌人，也就是说我方为优势，敌方为劣势。能以优势进攻劣势，那么与我决战的敌人就显得少了。

吾所与战之地不可知，（不可知）则敌所备者多；敌所备者多，则吾所与战者寡矣。

我所与敌决战的地点不为人知，那么敌人设防之处就会增多；敌人设防之处增多，那么与我决战的敌人就会减少。

故备前则后寡，备后则前寡，备左则右寡，备右则左寡，无所不备，则无所不寡。

所以前面设防则后面虚懈，后面设防则前面虚懈，左翼设防则右翼虚懈，右翼设防则左翼虚懈，到处设防则到处虚懈。

寡者，备人者也；众者，使之备己者也。

劣势，是防备别人的一方；优势，是使别人防备自己的一方。

Chapter 6: Weak Points and Strong Points

vided. If our army is united as one and the enemy's is fragmented, in using the undivided whole to attack his one, we are many to his few. If we are able to use many to strike few, anyone we take the battle to will be in desperate circumstances.

The place we have chosen to give the enemy battle must be kept from him. If he cannot anticipate us, the positions the enemy must prepare to defend will be many. And if the positions he must prepare to defend are many, then any unit we engage in battle will be few in number.

Thus if the enemy makes preparations by reinforcing his numbers at the front, his rear is weakened; if he makes preparations at the rear, his front is weakened; if he makes them on his left flank, his right is weakened; if he makes them on his right flank, his left is weakened. To be prepared everywhere is to be weak everywhere.

One is weak because he makes preparations against others; he has strength because he makes other prepare against him.

虚实第六

故知战之地，知战之日，则可千里而会战；不知战地，不知战日，则左不能救右，右不能救左，前不能救后，后不能救前，而况远者数十里，近者数里乎！

所以知道会战地点和会战时间，才能千里行军前往会战；不知道会战地点和会战时间，就会左翼不能救援右翼，右翼不能救援左翼，前面不能救援后面，后面不能救援前面，更何况是只有数十里或数里远近呢！

3. 以吾度之，越人之兵虽多，亦奚益于胜哉！

依我看来，越国人的兵力虽多，对它的取胜又有什么帮助呢？

4. 故曰：胜可为也，敌虽众，可使无斗。

所以说：胜利是可以争取的，敌人再多也可以让它停止战斗。

故策之而知得失之计，（作）〔候〕之而知动静之理，形之而知死生之地，角之而知有余不足之处。

所以通过运筹决策可以知道双方的得算多少，通过刺探敌情可以知道敌人的动静虚实，通过陈师部列可以知道地形的死生之势；通过实际较量可以知道双方的兵力众寡。

Chapter 6: Weak Points and Strong Points

Thus if one can anticipate the place and the day of battle, he can march a thousand *li* to join the battle. But if one cannot anticipate either the place or the day of battle, his left flank cannot even rescue his right, or his right his left; his front cannot even rescue his rear, or his rear his front. How much more is this so when your reinforcements are separated by at least a few *li*, or even tens of *li*.

3. The way I estimate it, even though the troops of Yüeh are many, what good is this to them in respect to victory?

4. Thus it is said: Victory can be created. For even though the enemy has the strength of numbers, we can prevent him from fighting us.

Therefore, analyze the enemy's battle plan to understand its merits and its weaknesses; provoke him to find out the pattern of his movements; make him show himself (*hsing*) to discover the viability of his battle position; skirmish with him to find out where he is strong and where he is vulnerable.

虚实第六

故形兵之极，至于无形。无形则深间不能窥，智者不能谋。因形而措胜于众，众不能知。人皆知我所以胜之形，而莫知吾所以制胜之形，故其战胜不复，而应形于无穷。

所以部署兵力的最高水平，是达到无形可见。无形可见则潜伏再深的间谍也无法刺探，足智多谋的人也无法揣测。运用分散集结的变化引导士兵夺取胜利，士兵无法了解。人们都知道我取得胜利的态势，却不知道我是怎样造成这种胜利态势的，所以每次作战取胜都不会重复旧的方法，总是能顺应各种形势变化而不断地变换战术。

5. （夫）兵形象水，水之（形）〔行〕避高而趋下，兵之形避实而击虚；水因地而制（流）〔行〕，兵因敌而制胜。

军队的态势好像流水，水的流动总是从高处流向低处，军队的态势总是避开敌人的坚实之处而进攻其虚懈之处；流水是根据地势而决定流向，军队也是因敌而制胜。

故兵无常势，水无常形。能因敌变化而取胜者，谓之神。

所以军队没有固定不变的态势，流水没有固定不变的形状。能够根据敌人的变化去夺取胜利的人，叫做"神"。

Chapter 6: Weak Points and Strong Points

The ultimate skill in taking up a strategic position (*hsing*) is to have no form (*hsing*). If your position is formless (*hsing*), the most carefully concealed spies will not be able to get a look at it, and the wisest counselors will not be able to lay plans against it. I present the rank and file with victories gained through (*yin*) strategic positioning (*hsing*), yet they are not able to understand them. Everyone knows the position (*hsing*) that has won me victory, yet none fathom how I came to settle on this winning position (*hsing*). Thus one's victories in battle cannot be repeated – they take their form (*hsing*) in response to inexhaustibly changing circumstances.

5. The positioning (*hsing*) of troops can be likened to water: Just as the flow of water avoids high ground and rushes to the lowest point, so on the path to victory avoid the enemy's strong points and strike where he is weak. As water varies its flow according to (*yin*) the fall of the land, so an army varies its method of gaining victory according to (*yin*) the enemy.

Thus an army does not have fixed strategic advantages (*shih*) or an invariable position (*hsing*). To be able to take the victory by varying one's position according to (*yin*) the enemy's is

虚实第六

故五行无常胜，四时无常位，日有短长，月有死生。

所以五行没有固定的相克，四季没有固定的位置，白昼有长有短，月亮有盈有亏。

Chapter 6: Weak Points and Strong Points

called being inscrutable (*shen*).

Thus, of the five phases (*wu xing*), none is the constant victor; of the four seasons, none occupies a constant position; the days are both short and long; the moon waxes and wanes.

军争第七

"军争"，指两军争夺会战的先机之利，即先敌到达会战地点，取得作战的有利条件。

作者认为，在战争全过程中，军争难度最大，包含许多矛盾。如你要先敌到达，从表面上看似乎以抄近道为最便捷，但抄近道会暴露意图，遭敌阻截；你要携带全部辎重争利就会赶不上，但没有辎重军队也无法生存。此外，还有像如何照顾行军动作的协调一致，如何保持士气、心理、体力上的优势，以及如何防敌有诈等等，往往很难处理。正是注意到这些矛盾，所以作者认为"军争之法"应当"以迂为直，以患为利"。

Chapter 7:
Armed Contest

军争第七

1. 孙子曰：

   凡用兵之法，将受命于君，合军聚众，交和而舍，莫难于军争。军争之难者，以迂为直，以患为利。

   孙子说：

   一般的用兵方法，从将领受命于君主，征集军队，到两军对垒，没有比"军争"（两军争利）更困难的。"军争"的困难，在于把弯路当作直路，把患害当作有利。

2. 故迂其途而诱之以利，后人发，先人至，此知迂直之计者也。

   所以采取迂回的路线并诱敌以利，比敌人晚出发，但比敌人先到达，这才是懂得弯路和直路两者的关系。

   军争为利，（众）〔军〕争为危。举军而争利则不及，委军而争利则辎重捐。是故卷甲而趋，日夜不处，倍道兼行，百里而争利，则擒三将军，劲者先，疲者后，其法十一而至；五十里而争利，则蹶上将军，其法半至；三十里而争利，则三分之二至。是故军无辎重则亡，无粮食则亡，无委积则亡。

   军争既有其利也有其害。携带全部辎重与敌争利就会赶不上，放弃全部辎重与敌争利就会损失辎重。所以卷起铠甲

Chapter 7: Armed Contest

1. Master Sun said:

    The art of using troops is this: In the process of the commander's receiving his orders from the ruler, assembling his armies, mobilizing the population for war, and setting up his camp facing the enemy, there is nothing of comparable difficulty to the armed contest itself. What is difficult in the armed contest is to turn the long and tortuous route into the direct, and to turn adversity into advantage.

2. Thus, making the enemy's road long and tortuous, lure him along it by baiting him with easy gains. Set out after he does, yet arrive before him. This is to understand the tactic of converting the tortuous and the direct.

    Armed contest can be both a source of advantage and of danger. If you mobilize your entire force to contend for some advantage, you arrive too late; if you abandon your base camp to contend for advantage, your equipment and stores will be lost. For this reason, if an army were to stow its armor and set off in haste, and stopping neither day nor night, force-march at double time for a hundred *li* to contend for some advantage, its commanders would all be taken, its strongest men would be out

军争第七

赶路，日夜不停，加倍赶路，走一百里路与敌争利，那么三军将领就可能全部被俘，士兵体力充沛的跑在前面，疲惫的落在后面，通常只有十分之一可以按期到达；走五十里路与敌争利，会折损上将军，通常只有一半可以按期到达；走三十里路与敌争利，通常只有三分之二可以按期到达。所以军队没有辎重会灭亡，没有粮食会灭亡，没有储备会灭亡。

3. 故不知诸侯之谋者，不能豫交；不知山林、险阻、沮泽之形者，不能行军；不用乡导者，不能得地利。

所以不了解各国诸侯的打算，不能预为结交；不了解山林、险阻、沼泽等地形，不能行军；不使用向导，不能得地利。

故兵以诈立，以利动，以分合为变者也。

所以军队是靠权诈而存在，视条件有利而行动，以分散集结为变化。

Chapter 7: Armed Contest

in front, the exhausted ones would lag behind, and as a rule only one tenth of its strength would reach the target.

Were it to travel fifty *li* at such a pace to contend for some advantage, the commander of the advance force would be lost, and as a rule only half of its strength would reach the target. Were it to travel thirty *li* at such a pace to contend for some advantage, only two thirds of its strength would reach the target. For this reason, if any army is without its equipment and stores, it will perish; if it is without provisions, it will perish; if it is without its material support, it will perish.

3. Therefore, unless you know the intentions of the rulers of the neighboring states, you cannot enter into preparatory alliances with them; unless you know the lay of the land – its mountains and forests, its passes and natural hazards, its wetlands and swamps – you cannot deploy the army on it; unless you can employ local scouts, you cannot turn the terrain to your advantage.

Therefore, in warfare rely on deceptive maneuvers to establish your ground, calculate advantages in deciding your movements, and divide up and consolidate your forces to make your strategic changes.

故其疾如风，其徐如林，侵掠如火，不动如山，难知如阴，动如雷震。

所以它快起来像风，慢起来像林，四出抄掠像火，按兵不动像山，难以窥测像阴天，突然发动像雷击。

掠乡分众，廓地分利，悬权而动。

抄掠乡村，分其民众；扩大土地，分其物产；权衡利害，相机而动。

先知迂直之计者胜，此军争之法也。

谁先掌握了以迂为直的奥妙谁就能获胜，这就是"军争"的方法。

4. 《军政》曰："言不相闻，故为之金鼓；视不相见，故为之旌旗。"夫金鼓旌旗者，所以一（人）〔民〕之耳目也。（人）〔民〕既专一，则勇者不得独进，怯者不得独退，此用众之法也。故夜战多（火）〔金〕鼓，昼战多旌旗，所以变人之耳目也。

《军政》说："说话听不到，所以设置金鼓（铜的打击乐器和鼓）；眼睛看不到，所以设置旌旗。"金鼓和旌旗，是用

Chapter 7: Armed Contest

Thus, advancing at a pace, such an army is like the wind; slow and majestic, it is like a forest; invading and plundering, it is like fire; sedentary, it is like a mountain; unpredictable, it is like a shadow; moving, it is like lightning and thunder.

In plundering the countryside, divide up your numbers; in extending your territory, divide up and hold the strategic positions; weigh the pros and cons before moving into action.

He who first understands the tactic of converting the tortuous and the direct will take the victory. This is the art of armed contest.

4. *The Book of Military Policies* states: It is because commands cannot be heard in the din of battle that drums and gongs are used; it is because units cannot identify each other in battle that flags and pennants are used. Thus, in night battle make extensive use of torches and drums, and in battle during the day make extensive use of flags and pennants. Drums, gongs, flags, and pennants are the way to coordinate the ears and eyes of the

军争第七

来统一人民的视听。人民的视听既然统一起来，那么勇敢的人也不能擅自前进，怯懦的人也不能擅自后退，这是指挥军队的方法。所以夜间作战以使用金鼓为主，白天作战以使用旌旗为主，好让人们能够交替使用他们的耳朵和眼睛。

5. 三军可夺气，将军可夺心。是故朝气锐，昼气惰，暮气归。善用兵者，避其锐气，击其惰归，此治气者也。

　　三军可以削弱其士气，将军可以沮丧其意志。所以早晨士气最盛，白天士气低落，傍晚士气衰竭。善于用兵的人，应避开其旺盛之时，而在其低落衰竭之时进攻，这是掌握士气。

　　以治待乱，以静待哗，此治心者也。

　　以整齐对付混乱，以安静对付喧哗，这是掌握心理。

　　以近待远，以佚待劳，以饱待饥，此治力者也。

　　以近便对付迂远，以安逸对付疲劳，以饱食对付饥饿，这是掌握体力。

　　无邀正正之旗，勿击堂堂之陈，此治变者也。

　　不要向旗帜整齐的军队挑战，不要向庞大的阵容进攻，

Chapter 7: Armed Contest

men. Once the men have been consolidated as one body, the courageous will not have to advance alone, and the cowardly will not get to retreat alone. This is the art of employing large numbers of troops.

5. An entire enemy army can be demoralized, and its commander can be made to lose heart. Now, in the morning of the way, the enemy's morale is high; by noon, it begins to flag; by evening, it has drained away. Thus the expert in using the military avoids the enemy when his morale is high, and strikes when his morale has flagged and has drained away. This is the way to manage morale.

Use your proper order to await the enemy's disorder; use your calmness to await his clamor. This is the way to manage the heart—and—mind.

Use your closeness to the battlefield to await the far—off enemy; use your well—rested troops to await his fatigued; use your well—fed troops to await his hungry. This is the way to manage strength.

Do not intercept an enemy that is perfectly uniform in its array of banners; do not launch the attack on an enemy that is full

这是防敌有变。

6. 故用兵之法，高陵勿向，背丘勿逆，佯北勿从，锐卒勿攻，饵兵勿食，归师勿遏，围师必阙，穷寇勿迫，此用兵之法也。

　　所以用兵的方法，敌军据守高山不可仰攻，背靠丘陵不可迎击，假装逃跑不可追击，士卒精锐不可进攻，佯动诱我不可中计，回家的敌军不可阻截，被围的敌军必留生路，陷于绝境的敌军不可逼迫，这就是用兵的方法。

Chapter 7: Armed Contest

and disciplined in its formations. This is the way to manage changing conditions.

6. Therefore, the art of using troops is this:

   Do not attack an enemy who has the high ground; do not go against an enemy that has his back to a hill; do not follow an enemy that feigns retreat; do not attack the enemy's finest; do not swallow the enemy's bait; do not obstruct an enemy returning home; in surrounding the enemy, leave him a way out; do not press an enemy that is cornered. This is the art of using troops.

九变第八

本篇所谓"九变",历来说法不一,如:今按"九变"实即《九地》"九地之变"。根据是:(1)本篇开头十句,前五句有四句与《九地》所述"九地之变"重出,"绝地无留"一句虽不直接见于《九地》,但"绝地"之名亦见于《九地》,与"衢"、"重"、"轻"、"围"、"死"并列。另外,《九地》"争地吾将趋其后",简本作"争地吾将使不留",有"不留"出现,可见也是从《九地》脱出;(2)本篇第二段"故将通于九变之利者,知用兵矣;将不通九变之利,虽知地形,不能得地之利矣"。"九变之利"即指"地之利",也正合"九地之变"。我们认为此篇系由《九地》割裂而出。

Chapter 8:
Adapting to the Nine
Contingencies (pien)

九变第八

1. 孙子曰：

   凡用兵之法，将受命于君，合军聚众，圮地无舍，衢地合交，绝地无留，围地则谋，死地则战。途有所不由，军有所不击，城有所不攻，地有所不争，君命有所不受。

   孙子说：

   一般的用兵方法，将领受命于君主，征集军队，在圮地不可宿营，在衢地要四面结交，在绝地不可滞留，在围地要巧设计谋，在死地要决一死战。有的道路并不一定要经过，有的军队并不一定要出击，有的城池并不一定要攻打，有的地利并不一定要争夺，有的君命并不一定要执行。

2. 故将通于九变之利者，知用兵矣；将不通九变之利，虽知地形，不能得地之利矣；治兵不知九变之术，虽知五利，不能得人之用矣。

   所以将领通晓"九变"的好处，算是懂得用兵；将领不通晓"九变"的好处，即使熟悉地形，也不能得到地利；带兵不懂"九变"的运用方法，即使懂得"五利"，也不能充分发挥军队的作用。

3. 是故智者之虑，必杂于利害，杂于利而务可信也，杂于害而

Chapter 8: Adapting to the Nine Contingencies

1. Master Sun said:

   The art of using troops is this: When the commander receives his orders from the ruler, assembles his armies, and mobilizes the population for war, he should not make camp on difficult terrain; he should join with his allies on strategically vital intersections; he should not linger on cutoff terrain; he should have contingency plans on terrain vulnerable to ambush; and he should take the fight to the enemy on terrain from which there is no way out. There are roadways not to be traveled, armies not to be attacked, walled cities not to be assaulted, territory not to be contested, and commands from the ruler not to be obeyed.

2. Thus, a commander fully conversant with the advantages to be gained in adapting to these nine contingencies will know how to employ troops; a commander who is not, even if he knows the lay of the land, will not be able to use it to his advantage. One who commands troops without knowing the art of adapting to these nine contingencies, even if he knows the five advantages, will not be able to get the most from his men.

3. For this reason, the deliberations of the wise commander are

九变第八

患可解也。

所以聪明的人考虑问题，一定要兼顾利、害两个方面，见害而思利，事情方可进展；见利而思害，危难方可排除。

是故屈诸侯者以害，役诸侯者以业，趋诸侯者以利。

所以屈服诸侯是靠损害，役使诸侯是靠实力，调动诸侯是靠利诱。

故用兵之法，无恃其不来，恃吾有以待之；无恃其不攻，恃吾有所不可攻也。

所以用兵的方法，不是靠敌人不来，而是靠我有对付敌人的办法；不是靠敌人不进攻，而是靠我凤有准备，使敌人无法进攻。

4. 故将有五危：必死可杀，必生可虏，忿速可侮，廉洁可辱，爱民可烦。凡此五者，将之过也，用兵之灾也。覆军杀将，必以五危，不可不察也。

所以将领有五大危险：只知拚命就会被杀死，一味贪生就会被俘虏，忿怒急切就会被挑逗，爱重名节就会被侮辱，溺爱其民就会被烦扰。所有这五种危险，都是将领的过失，

sure to assess jointly both advantages and disadvantages. In taking full account of what is advantageous, he can fulfill his responsibilities; in taking full account of what is disadvantageous, his difficulties become resolvable.

For this reason, to subjugate neighboring states, use the threat of injury; to keep them in service, drive them on; to lure them out, use the prospect of gain.

The art of using troops is this:

Do not depend on the enemy not coming; depend rather on being ready for him. Do not depend on the enemy not attacking; depend rather on having a position that cannot be attacked.

4. There are five traits that are dangerous in a commander: If he has a reckless disregard for life, he can be killed; if he is determined to live at all costs, he can be captured; if he has a volatile temper, he can be provoked; if he is a man of uncompromising honor, he is open to insult; if he loves his people, he can be easily troubled and upset. These five traits are generally faults in a commander, and can prove disastrous in the conduct of

九变第八

用兵的灾害。全军覆没，将领被杀，必定是由于这五种危险，不可不加以了解。

Chapter 8: Adapting to the Nine Contingencies

war. Since an army's being routed and its commander slain is invariably the consequence of these five dangerous traits, they must be given careful consideration.

行军第九

本篇着重讲行军中的宿营（"处军"）和观察敌情（"相敌"）两个问题。前者分"处山"、"处水"、"处斥泽"、"处平陆"四大类，后者包括三十三种情况。

Chapter 9:
Deploying the Army

行军第九

1. 孙子曰：

   凡处军相敌：

   孙子说：

   宿营和观察敌情包括：

   绝山依谷，视生处高，战（隆）〔降〕无登，此处山之
军也。

   穿越山地，要依傍谷地；面向开阔，依托高地；与自高
而下的敌军交战，不可登山仰攻，这是在山地的宿营。

   绝水必远水。客绝水而来，勿迎之于水内，令半渡而击
之利；欲战者，无附于水而迎客；视生处高，无迎水流，此
处水上之军也。

   穿越水域，一定要远离水边；敌若渡水而来，不可迎战
于水中，要让敌人渡至一半再出击才有利；若欲交战，不可
贴近水边而迎战敌人，要面向开阔，依托高地，这是在水域
的宿营。

   绝斥泽，唯亟去无留；若交军于斥泽之中，必依水草而
背众树，此处斥泽之军也。

Chapter 9: Deploying the Army

1. Master Sun said:

In positioning your armies and assessing the enemy:

Pass through the mountains keeping to the valleys; pitch camp on high ground facing the sunny side; and joining battle in the hills, do not ascend to engage the enemy. This is positioning an army when in the mountains.

Crossing water, you must move to distance yourself from it. When the invading army crosses water in his advance, do not meet him in the water. It is to your advantage to let him get halfway across and then attack him. Wanting to join the enemy in battle, do not meet his invading force near water. Take up a position on high ground facing the sunny side that is not downstream from the enemy. This is positioning an army when near water.

Crossing salt marshes, simply get through them in all haste and without delay. If you engage the enemy's force on the salt marshes, you must take your position near grass and water and

行军第九

穿越咸滩，必须迅速通过，不可停留；如果交战于咸滩中，一定要依傍水草而背靠树林，这是在咸滩的宿营。

平陆处易，右背高，前死后生，此处平陆之军也。

在平原上，要宿营于平坦之处，右侧和背面为高地，前面为死地，后面为生地，这是在平原的宿营。

凡四军之利，黄帝之所以胜四帝也。

掌握了这四种地形上宿营的便利，是黄帝战胜〔青、赤、白、黑〕四帝的原因。

凡军好高而恶下，贵阳而贱阴。养生处实，军无百疾，是谓必胜。丘陵堤防，必处其阳而右背之，此兵之利，地之助也。

一般都喜欢选择高地而不喜欢选择低地，喜欢选择阳面而不喜欢选择阴面。凭借水草之利养生，依托可靠的地形宿营，军队中没有各种疫病流行，这样才有必胜的把握。碰到丘陵和堤岸，一定要宿营于其阳面，右侧和背面对着它。这对用兵有利，全靠地形的帮助。

上雨水，〔水〕（沫）〔流〕至，欲涉者，待其定也。

with your back to the woods. This is positioning an army when on salt marshes.

On the flatlands, position yourself on open ground, with your right flank backing on high ground, and with dangerous ground in front and safe ground behind. This is positioning an army when on flatlands.

Gaining the advantageous position for his army in these four different situations was the way the Yellow Emperor defeated the emperors of the four quarters.

Generally speaking, an army prefers high ground and dislikes the low, prizes the sunny side and shuns the shady side, seeks a place in which food and water are readily available and ample to supply its needs, and wants to be free of he numerous diseases. These conditions mean certain victory. Encountering rises, hills, embankments, and dikes, you must position yourself on the sunny side and on your right flank have your back to the slope. This is an advantage for the troops, and is exploiting whatever help the terrain affords.

When it is raining upstream and churning waters descend,

行军第九

上游下雨，水流冲下，若涉水，要等水势稳定。

凡地有绝涧、天井、天牢、天罗、天陷、天隙，必亟去
之，勿近也。吾远之，敌近之；吾迎之，敌背之。

凡是碰上绝涧、天井、天牢、天罗、天陷、天隙等地
形，一定要迅速离开，不可接近。我必远离它，而使敌人接
近它，我必面对它，而使敌人背对它。

军旁有险阻、潢井、蒹葭、(林木)〔小林〕、翳荟者，必
谨覆索之，此伏奸之所〔处〕也。

军营附近如果有险阻、沼泽、芦苇、矮树和茂密的草
丛，务必细心搜索，这些地方往往是藏伏奸细之处。

2. 〔敌〕近而静者，恃其险也。

敌与我接近而毫无动静，是因为有险可恃。

远而挑战者，欲人之进也。

与我远离却向我挑战，是为了激我前往。

其所居 (易者)〔者易〕，利也。

Chapter 9: Deploying the Army

do not try to cross, but wait for the waters to subside.

Encountering steep river gorges, natural wells, box canyons, dense ground cover, quagmires, or natural defiles, quit such places with haste. Do not approach them. In keeping our distance from them, we can maneuver the enemy near to them; in keeping them to our front, we can maneuver the enemy to have them at his back.

If the army is flanked by precipitous ravines, stagnant ponds, reeds and rushes, mountain forests, and tangled undergrowth, these places must be searched carefully and repeatedly, for they are where ambushes are laid and spies are hidden.

2. If the enemy is close and yet quiet,
    He occupies a strategic position;

    If he is at a distance and yet acts provocatively,
    He wants us to advance.

    Where he has positioned himself on level ground,

行军第九

其所居之地地势低平，是占有地利。

众树动者，来也。

树丛枝叶摇动，是有敌前来。

众草多障者，疑也。

草丛之中多设障碍，是制造假象。

鸟起者，伏也。

鸟惊飞，是有埋伏。

兽骇者，覆也。

兽骇走，是有偷袭。

尘高而锐者，车来也。

路土高而尖，是有战车来。

卑而广者，徒来也。

路土低而宽，是有步兵来。

Chapter 9: Deploying the Army

He is harboring some advantage;

If there is movement in the trees,
He is coming;

If there are many blinds in the bushes,
He is looking to confuse us;

If birds take no flight,
He is lying in ambush;

If animals stampede in fear,
He is mounting a surprise attack;

If the dust peaks up high,
His chariots are coming;

If the dust spreads out low to the ground,
His infantry is coming;

行军第九

散而条达者，樵采也。

路土散乱成条状，是打柴经过。

少而往来者，营军也。

路土少而有往来的痕迹，是要安营。

辞卑而益备者，进也。

敌人口气谦卑却加紧准备，是要进攻。

辞强而进驱者，退也。

口气强硬而佯装前进，是要撤退。

轻车先出居其侧者，陈也。

轻车先出位于其侧翼，是要布阵。

无约而请和者，谋也。

提出讲和却并无协议，是另有阴谋。

奔走而陈兵者，期也。

奔走布阵，是要集合。

Chapter 9: Deploying the Army

If the dust reaches out in scattered ribbons,
His firewood details have been dispatched;

If a few clouds of dust come and go,
He is making camp.

If his envoys are modest of word yet he continues to increase
his readiness for war,
He will advance;

If his language is belligerent and he advances aggressively,
He will withdraw;

If his light chariots move out first And take up position on
the flanks,
He is moving into formation;
If he has suffered no setback and yet sues for peace,
He is plotting;

If he moves rapidly with his troops in formation,
He is setting the time for battle;

半进半退者，诱也。

半进半退，是想引诱。

杖而立者，饥也。

士兵拄杖而立，是饿了。

汲而先饮者，渴也。

打水的人抢着先喝，是渴了。

见利而不进者，劳也。

见到好处却不肯前往，是累了。

鸟集者，虚也。

鸟雀落满，是空营虚设。

夜呼者，恐也。

半夜呼叫，是害怕。

军扰者，将不重也。

军中骚乱，是将领无威。

Chapter 9: Deploying the Army

If some of his troops advance and some retreat,

He is seeking to lure us forward.

If the enemy soldiers lean on their weapons,

They are hungry;

If those sent for water first drink themselves,

They are thirsty;

If there is an advantage to be had yet they do not advance to
secure it,

They are weary;

Where birds gather,

The enemy position is unoccupied;

Here there are shouts in the night,

The enemy is frightened;

Where there are disturbances in the ranks,

The enemy commander is not respected;

旌旗动者,乱也;

旌旗动摇,是混乱。

吏怒者,倦也。

军吏发怒,是疲倦。

杀马肉食者,军无粮也;

杀马吃肉,是军中无粮。

悬(瓴)〔甀〕不返其舍者,穷寇也。

悬挂瓶罐不回营舍,是陷于绝境的敌人。

谆谆谕谕,徐与人言者,失众也。

絮絮不休,慢声细语地与人讲话,是因为失去部下的拥护。

数赏者,窘也。

频繁地赏赐,是因为一筹莫展。

数罚者,困也;

Chapter 9: Deploying the Army

Where their flags and pennants are shifted about,
The enemy is in disorder;

Where his officers are easily angered,
The enemy is exhausted.

Where the enemy feeds his horses grain and his men meat,
And where his men no longer bother to hang up their water
vessels,

Or return to camp,
The now—desperate enemy is ready to fight to the death.

Where, hemming and hawking,
The enemy commander speaks to his subordinates in a meek
and halting voice,
He has lost his men.
Meting out too many rewards
Means the enemy is in trouble,

And meting out too many punishments

行军第九

频繁地惩罚，是因为陷入困境。

先暴而后畏其众者，不精之至也。

开始态度粗暴但后来又畏惧其部下，是极不精明。

来委谢者，欲休息也。

前来送礼谢罪，是打算暂时休战。

兵怒而相迎，久而不合，又不相去，必谨察之。

敌军怒气冲冲前来迎战，却总是不肯交锋，又不撤离，一定要细心观察。

3. **兵非贵益多，虽无武进，足以并力、料敌、取人而已。夫唯无虑而易敌者，必擒于人。卒未亲附而罚之，则不服，不服则难用。卒已亲附而罚不行，则不可用。故（令）〔合〕之以文，齐之以武，是谓必取。**

用兵并非人数愈多愈好，只求不轻举妄动，能够集中力量，判明敌情，取胜敌人而已。只有不加深思熟虑、一味轻敌的人，必定会被敌人擒获。所以尚未取得士兵的真心拥护就惩罚他们，他们就会不服，不服就难于使用。已经取得士

Chapter 9: Deploying the Army

Means he is in dire straits.

The commander who erupts violently at his subordinates,
Only then to fear them,
Is totally inept.

When the enemy's emissary comes with conciliatory words
He wants to end hostilities.

When an angry enemy confronts you for an extended time, without either joining you in battle or quitting his position, you must watch him with the utmost care.

3. In war it is not numbers that give the advantage. If you do not advance recklessly, and are able to consolidate your own strength, get a clear picture of the enemy's situation, and secure the full support of your men, it is enough. It is only the one who has no plan and takes his enemy lightly who is certain to be captured by him. I you punish troops who are not yet devoted to you, they will not obey, and if they do not obey, they are difficult to use. But once you have their devotion, if discipline

行军第九

兵的真心拥护而不能执行惩罚，便无法使用他们。所以用恩赏来使他们团结，用威罚来使他们整齐，这样才能必定取胜。

令素行以教其民，则民服；令（不素）〔素不〕行以教其民，则民不服。令素行者，与众相得也。

命令一贯顺利执行，用来训练其人民，人民就会服从；命令一贯不能.顺利执行，用来训练其人民，人民就会不服从。命令一贯顺利执行，是因为将领和士兵彼此都非常熟悉和信任。

Chapter 9: Deploying the Army

is not enforced, you cannot use them either. Therefore, bring them together by treating them humanely and keep them in line with strict military discipline. This will assure their allegiance.

If commands are consistently enforced in the training of the men, they will obey; if commands are not enforced in their training, they will not obey. The consistent enforcement of commands promotes a complimentary relationship between the commander and his men.

地形第十

本篇是讲六种形势特点不同的作战地形以及相应的战术要求。这里所谓"地形"主要是根据会战的要求，按攻守进退之便而划分，偏重形势特点。它与《行军》所述"处军"之地不同，"处军"之地是讲行军时的地形依托，偏重地貌；它与《九地》所述"九地"也不同，"九地"往往是从"主客"形势、深入程度这些角度去讲，偏重区域性的概念。

Chapter 10:
The Terrain

地形第十

1. 孙子曰：

   地形有通者，有挂者，有支者，有隘者，有险者，有远者。

   孙子说：

   地形有"通"、"挂"、"支"、"隘"、"险"、"远"六种。

   我可以往，彼可以来，曰通。通形者，先居高阳，利粮道，以战则利。

   我可以往，敌可以来，叫"通"。"通形"，应先占据地势较高并且向阳的地点，保证粮道畅通，这样作战才有利。

   可以往，难以返，曰挂。挂形者，敌无备，出而胜之，敌若有备，出而不胜，难以返，不利。

   可以前往，难以返回，叫"挂"。"挂形"，敌人没有戒备，可以出击战胜它，敌人如果有戒备，出击不胜，难以返回，则不利。

   我出而不利，彼出而不利，曰支。支形者，敌虽利我，我无出也，引而去之，令敌半出而击之利。

   我出击不利，敌出击也不利，叫"支"。"支形"，敌人即使引诱我，我也不要出击，而应调兵撤离，让敌人出动一半

Chapter 10: The Terrain

1. Master Sun said:

Kinds of terrain include the accessible, that which entangles, that which leads to a stand-off, the narrow pass, the precipitous defile and the distant.

Terrain that both armies can approach freely is called accessible. On accessible terrain, the army that enters the battle having been first to occupy high ground on the sunny side and to establish convenient supply lines, fights with the advantage.

Terrain that allows your advance but hampers your return is entangling. On entangling ground, if you go out and engage the enemy when he is not prepared, you might defeat him. But when the enemy is prepared, if you go out and engage him and fail to defeat him, you will be hard-pressed to get out, and will be in trouble.

Terrain that when entered disadvantages both our side and the enemy is ground that will lead to a stand-off. On this kind of terrain, even if the enemy tempts us out, we must not take the bait, but should quit the position and withdraw. Having lured

地形第十

后再出击才有利。

　　隘形者，我先居之，必盈之以待敌，若敌先居之，盈而勿从，不盈而从之。

　　"隘形"，我先占领，一定要完全控扼隘口以等待敌人，如果敌先占领，隘口完全被控扼就不要与敌接战，没有完全控扼则可与敌接战。

　　险形者，我先居之，必居高阳以待敌，若敌先居之，引而去之，勿从也。

　　"险形"，我先占领，一定要占据地势较高并且向阳的地点等待敌人，如果敌先占领，则调兵撤离，不可与敌接战。

　　远形者，势均，难以挑战，战而不利。

　　"远形"，双方形势均等，难以挑战，作战则不利。

　　凡此六者，地之道也，将之至任，不可不察也。

　　上述六种地形及其战术要求，是掌握地形的关键，将领负有重大责任，不可不加以了解。

Chapter 10: The Terrain

the enemy halfway out, we can then strike to our advantage.

With the narrow pass, if we can occupy it first, we must fully garrison it and await the enemy. When the enemy has occupied it first, if he garrisons it completely, do not follow him, but if he fails to, we can go after him.

With the precipitous defile, if we can occupy it first, we must take the high ground on the sunny side and await the enemy. Where the enemy has occupied it first, quit the position and withdraw, and do not follow him.

When the enemy is at some distance, if the strategic advantages of both sides are about the same, it is not easy to provoke him to fight, and taking the battle to him is not to our advantage.

Now these are the side guidelines (*tao*) governing the use of terrain. They are the commander's utmost responsibility, and must be thoroughly investigated.

地形第十

2. 故兵有走者，有弛者，有陷者，有崩者，有乱者，有北者。
凡此六者，非天地之灾，将之过也。

军队会出现"走"、"弛"、"陷"、"崩"、"乱"、"北"六
种情况。这六种情况，都不是由天地的灾害所造成，而是由
将领的过失所造成的。

夫势均，以一击十，曰走；

双方形势均等，以一击十，叫"走"；

卒强吏弱，曰弛；

士卒强悍而军吏懦弱，叫"弛"；

吏强卒弱，曰陷；

军吏强悍而士卒懦弱，叫"陷"；

大吏怒而不服，遇敌怼而自战，将不知其能，曰崩；

高级军吏愤怒而不听指挥，碰上仇敌擅自出战，将领又
不了解其能力，叫"崩"；

将弱不严，教道不明，吏卒无常，陈兵纵横，曰乱；

Chapter 10: The Terrain

2. In warfare there is flight, insubordination, deterioration, ruin, chaos, and rout. These six situations are not natural catastrophes but the fault of the commander.

When the strategic advantages of both sides are about the same, for an army to attack an enemy ten times its size will result in flight.

If the troops are strong but the officers weak, the result will be insubordination.

If the officers are strong but the troops weak, the result will be deterioration.

If your ranking officers are angry and insubordinate and, on encountering the enemy, allow their rancor to spur them into unauthorized engagements so that their commander does not know the strength of his own forces, the result will be ruin.

If the commander is weak and lax, his instructions and lead-

将领懦弱，管束不严，教导不明，军吏和士卒没有纪律约束，阵容不整，叫"乱"；

将不能料敌，以少合众，以弱击强，兵无选锋，曰北。

将领不能判断敌情，以劣势对付优势，以弱小进攻强大，军队缺乏精心挑选的前锋，叫"北"。

凡此六者，败之道也，将之至任，不可不察也。

这六种情况，是造成失败的关键，将领负有重大责任，不可不加以了解。

3. 夫地形者，兵之助也。料敌制胜，计险厄远近，上将之道也。知此而用战者必胜，不知此而用战者必败。

地形，是用兵的必要辅助条件。判断敌情，夺取胜利，估计地形的险隘和远近，这是上将的职责。知道这些去指挥作战就一定会胜利，不知道这些去指挥作战就一定会失败。

故战道必胜，主曰无战，必战可也；战道不胜，主曰必战，无战可也。

所以战场形势必然会取胜，君主说不要打，也可以坚决地打；战场形势不能取胜，君主说一定要打，也可以不打。

Chapter 10: The Terrain

ership unenlightened, his officers and troops undisciplined, and his military formations in disarray, the result will be chaos.

If the commander, unable to assess his enemy, sends a small force to engage a large one, sends his weak troops to attack the enemy's best, and operates without a vanguard of crack troops, the result will be rout.

These are six ways (*tao*) to certain defeat. They are the commander's utmost responsibility, and must be thoroughly investigated.

3. Strategic position (*hsing*) is an ally in battle. To assess the enemy's situation and create conditions that lead to victory, to analyze natural hazards and proximate distances – this is the way (*tao*) of the superior commander. He who fights with full knowledge of these factors is certain to win; he who fights without it is certain to lose.

Thus, if the way (*tao*) of battle guarantees your victory, it is right for you to insist on fighting even if the ruler has said not to; where the way (*tao*) of battle does not allow victory, it is right for you to refuse to fight even if the ruler has said you must.

地形第十

故进不求名，退不避罪，唯民是保，而利于主，国之宝也。

所以进不求功名，退不避罪责，只求保护人民，有利于君主，这是国家最宝贵的东西。

4. 视卒如婴儿，故可与之赴深溪；视卒如爱子，故可与之俱死。爱而不能令，厚而不能使，乱而不能治，譬如骄子，不可用也。

把士卒看做婴儿，所以可以与之共赴深溪；把士卒看做爱子，所以可以与之一起去死。溺爱而不能指挥，厚待而不能使用，混乱而不能惩治，好比骄子，是不能用来打仗的。

5. 知吾卒之可以击，而不知敌之不可击，胜之半也；知敌之可击，而不知吾卒之不可以击，胜之半也，知敌之可击，知吾卒之可以击，而不知地形之不可以战，胜之半也。

知道我之士卒可以用来进攻，而不知道敌人不可进攻，胜利的可能只有一半；知道敌人可以进攻，而不知道我之士卒不可以用来进攻，胜利的可能只有一半；知道敌人可以进攻，也知道我之士卒可以进攻，而不知道地形不可以用来作

Chapter 10: The Terrain

___

Hence a commander who advances without any thought of wining personal fame and withdraws in spite of certain punishment, whose only concern is to protect his people and promote the interests of his ruler, is the nation's treasure.

4. Because he fusses over his men as if they were infants, they will accompany him into the deepest valleys; because he fusses over his men as if they were his own beloved sons, they will die by his side. If he is generous with them and yet they do not do as he tells them, if he loves them and yet they do not obey his commands, if he is so undisciplined with them that he cannot bring them into proper order, they will be like spoiled children who can be put to no good use at all.

5. To know our troops can attack yet be unaware that the enemy is not open t attack, reduces our chances of victory to half; to know the enemy is open to attack and yet be unaware that our own troops cannot attack, reduces our chances of victory again to half; to know the enemy is open to attack and our troops can attack, and yet be unaware that the terrain does not favor us in battle, reduces the chances of victory once again to half.

战，胜利的可能也只有一半。

故知兵者，动而不迷，举而不穷。

所以懂得用兵的人，举动清醒不惑，措施变化无穷。

故曰：知彼知己，胜乃不殆；知天知地，胜乃可全。

所以说：知道敌人也知道自己，胜利才确有把握；知道天时也知道地利，胜利才万无一失。

Chapter 10: The Terrain

Thus when one who understands war moves, he does not go the wrong way, and when he takes action, he does not reach a dead end.

Hence it is said:

Know the other, know yourself,

And the victory will not be at risk;

Know the ground, know the natural conditions,

And the victory can be total.

九地第十一

本篇所述"九地"可分三类：（1）是从
"主客"形势（在己国为"主"，在敌国为
"客"）和深入程度的角度讲，有"散地"
（在己国）、"轻地"（在敌国，进入不深）、
"重地"（在敌国，进入深）、"交地"（与敌
国相交之地）、"衢地"（与多国相交之地）；
（2）是从行军的角度讲，有"圮地"（难行
之地）；（3）是从会战的角度讲，有"争
地"（两军相争之地），"围地"（被围之
地）、"死地"（无可逃之地）。

Chapter 11:
The Nine Kinds of Terrain

九地第十一

1. 孙子曰：

   用兵之法：有散地，有轻地，有争地，有交地，有衢地，有重地，有圮地，有围地，有死地。

   孙子说：

   用兵的方法：有散地，有轻地，有争地，有交地，有衢地，有重地，有圮地，有围地，有死地。

   诸侯自战其地者，为散地。

   诸侯在自己的国土上作战，叫散地。

   入人之地而不深者，为轻地。

   进入敌境不深，叫轻地。

   我得亦利，彼得亦利者，为争地。

   我占据有利，敌占据也有利，叫争地。

   我可以往，彼可以来者，为交地。

   我可以往，敌可以来，叫交地。

   诸侯之地三属，先至而得天下之众者，为衢地。

Chapter 11: The Nine Kinds of Terrain

1. Master Sun said:

   In the art of employing troops, the kinds of terrain include scattering terrain, marginal terrain, contested terrain, intermediate terrain, the strategically vital intersection, critical terrain, difficult terrain, terrain vulnerable to ambush, and terrain from which there is no way out.

   Where a feudal ruler does battle within his own territory, it is a terrain that permits the scattering of his troops.

   Where one has penetrated only barely into enemy territory, it is marginal terrain.

   Ground that gives us or the enemy the advantage in occupying it is contested terrain.

   Ground accessible to both sides is intermediate terrain.

   The territory of several neighboring states at which their bor-

九地第十一

诸侯的国土与多国接壤，先到达者可以得到天下之众，叫衢地。

入人之地深，背城邑多者，为重地。

进入敌境深，所过城邑多，叫重地。

山林，险阻、沮泽，凡难行之道者，为圮地。

凡山林、险阻、沼泽，一切难行之道，叫圮地。

所由入者隘，所从归者迂，彼寡可以击吾之众者，为围地。

入口狭窄，归路迂曲，敌人用劣势兵力可以攻击我之优势兵力，叫围地。

疾战则存，不疾战则亡者，为死地。

速战速决就能生存，不速战速决就会灭亡，叫死地。

是故散地则无战，轻地则无止，争地则无攻，交地则无绝，衢地则合交，重地则掠，圮地则行，围地则谋，死地则战。

所以散地不可作战，轻地不可停留，争地不可主动进攻，交地不可首尾脱节，衢地应当广结交援，重地应当四出

Chapter 11: The Nine Kinds of Terrain

ders meet is a strategically vital intersection. The first to reach it will gain the allegiance of the other states of the empire.

When an army has penetrated deep into enemy territory, and has many of the enemy's walled cities and towns at its back, it is on critical terrain.

Mountains and forests, passes and natural hazards, wetlands and swamps, and any such roads difficult to traverse constitute difficult terrain.

Ground that gives access through a narrow defile, and where exit is tortuous, allowing an enemy in small numbers to attack our main force, is terrain vulnerable to ambush.

Ground on which you will survive only if you fight with all your might, but will perish if you fail to do so, is terrain with no way out.

This being the case, do not fight on scattering terrain; do not stay on marginal terrain; do not attack the enemy on contested terrain; do not get cut off on intermediate terrain; form alliances with the neighboring states at strategically vital intersections;

抄掠，圮地应当迅速通过，围地应当设计突围，死地应当拼死一战。

2. 古之善用兵者，能使敌人前后不相及，众寡不相恃，贵贱不相救，上下不相收，卒离而不集，兵合而不齐。

　　古代善于用兵的人，能使敌人前面和后面不相衔接，主力和非主力不相呼应，身份高贵者和低贱者不相援救，上级和下级不相统属，士卒分散了便无法集中，兵力集中了也不能整齐。

　　合于利而动，不合于利而止。敢问敌众（整而）〔而整〕将来，待之若何？曰：先夺其所爱则听矣。

　　合于利而行动，不合于利则停止。试问：如果敌人人多势众，阵容严整，将要前来与我作战，应当怎样对付？答案是：先夺取其要害就能使其就范。

Chapter 11: The Nine Kinds of Terrain

plunder the enemy's resources on critical terrain; press ahead on difficult terrain; devise contingency plans on terrain vulnerable to ambush; and on terrain from which there is no way out, take the battle to the enemy.

2. The commanders of old said to be expert at the use of the military were able to ensure that which the enemy:

His vanguard and rearguard could not relieve each other,

The main body of his army and its special detachments could not support each other,

Officers and men could not come to each other's aid,

And superiors and subordinates could not maintain their lines of communication.

The enemy forces when scattered could not regroup,

And when their army assembled, it could not form ranks.

If it was to the advantage of these expert commanders, they would move into action; if not, they would remain in place. Suppose I am asked: If the enemy, in great numbers and with strict discipline in the ranks, is about to advance on us, how do we deal with him? I would reply: If you get ahead of him to seize something he cannot afford to lose, he will do your bidding.

兵之情主速，乘人之不及，由不虞之道，攻其所不戒也。

用兵的诀窍是靠行动迅速，乘敌人尚未赶到，由意想不到的路线，去进攻它所不曾防备的地方。

3. 凡为客之道，深入则专，主人不克；掠于饶野，三军足食。谨养而勿劳，并气积力；运兵计谋，为不可测。

一般进入敌国作战的要求是，深入则意志专一，令守敌无法抵御；抄掠其富饶的乡村，使三军有充足的粮食；小心保养，勿使劳累，鼓足士气，积聚力量；调动兵力，制订计谋，使敌人虚实莫测。

4. 投之无所往，死且不北。死焉不得，士人尽力。

把士兵投入无路可走的境地，他们就会宁可战死也不逃跑。战死已成求之不得，士兵就会竭尽全力。

兵士甚陷则不惧，无所往则固，入深则拘，不得已则

Chapter 11 : The Nine Kinds of Terrain

War is such that the supreme consideration is speed. This is to take advantage of what is beyond the reach of the enemy, to go by way of routes where he least expects you, and to attack where he has made no preparations.

3. The general methods of operation (*tao*) for an invading army are:

The deeper you penetrate into enemy territory, the greater the cohesion of your troops, and the less likely the host army will prevail over you.

Plunder the enemy's most fertile fields, and your army will have ample provisions.

Attend to the nourishment of your troops and do not let them get worn down; lift their morale and build up their strength.

Deploy your troops and plan out your strategies in such a way that the enemy cannot fathom your movements.

4. Throw your troops into situations from which there is no way out, and they will choose death over desertion. Once they are ready to die, how could you get less than maximum exertion from your officers and men?

Even where your troops are in the most desperate straits,

九地第十一

斗。是故其兵不修而戒，不求而得，不约而亲，不令而信，禁祥去疑，至死无所之。

士兵陷入困境过深就会无所畏惧，无路可逃就会军心稳固，深入敌境就会紧张拘束，迫不得已就会拼死搏斗。所以这样的军队不用调教也会戒备，不用要求也会执行，不用约束也会亲附，不用命令也会服从，禁绝吉凶占验，祛除疑惑忧虑，就是战死也不会退逃。

5. 吾士无余财，非恶货也；无余命，非恶寿也。令发之日，士卒坐者涕沾襟，偃卧者涕交颐，投之无所往，诸、刿之勇也。

我方士兵肯弃财货于不顾，不是因为讨厌财货；敢舍性命于一死，不是因为讨厌寿命。命令下达之日，士兵们坐着的涕泪沾湿衣衫，躺着的涕泪淌过腮边，只要把他们投入无

Chapter 11: The Nine Kinds of Terrain

They will have no fear,

And with nowhere else to turn,

They will stand firm;

Having penetrated deep into enemy territory,

They are linked together,

And if need be,

They will fight.

For this reason, with no need of admonishment, they are
vigilant;

Without compulsion, they carry out their duties;

Without tying them down, they are devoted;

With no need for orders, they follow army discipline.

Proscribe talk of omens and get rid of rumors,

And even to the death they will not retreat.

5. Our soldiers do not have an abundance of wealth, but it is not
because they despise worldly goods; their life expectancy is not
long, but it is not because they despise longevity. On the day
these men are ordered into battle, those sitting have tears soak-
ing their collars, and those lying on their backs have tears cross-

路可走的境地，他们会像专诸、曹刿一样勇敢。

故善用兵者，譬如率然。率然者，常山之蛇也，击其首则尾至，击其尾则首至，击其中则首尾俱至。

所以善于用兵的人，就好比率然一样。率然，是常山（恒山）中的一种蛇，打它的头，它的尾巴就会来救应；打它的尾巴，它的头就调来救应，打它的身子，它的头和尾巴就会一起来救应。

敢问〔兵〕可使如率然乎？曰：可。夫吴人与越人相恶也，当其同舟济而遇风，其相救也如左右手。

试问能够使军队像率然一样吗？答案是可以。吴人和越人是相互仇视的，但当他们同乘一条船渡水而碰上风暴，他们互相救助竟像人的左右两手。

是故方马埋轮，未足恃也；齐勇若一，政之道也；刚柔皆得，地之理也。故善用兵者，携手若使一人，不得已也。

所以并联战马，掩埋车轮，是靠不住的；协调勇士与懦夫，有如一人，才是御兵之术的上乘；兼顾刚地与柔弱，相

Chapter 11: The Nine Kinds of Terrain

ing on their cheeks. But throw them into a situation where there is no way out and they will show the courage of any Chuan Chu or Ts'ao Kuei.

Therefore, those who are expert at employing the military are like the "sudden striker." The "sudden striker" is a snake indigenous to Mount Heng. If you strike its head, its tail comes to its aid; if you strike its tail, its head comes to its aid; if you strike its middle, both head and tail come to its aid.

Suppose I am asked: Can troops be trained to be like this "sudden striker" snake? I would reply: They can. The men of Wu and Yüeh hate each other. Yet if they were crossing the river in the same boat and were caught by gale winds, they would go to each other's aid like the right hand helping the left.

For this reason, it has never been enough to depend on tethered horses and buried chariot wheels. The object (*tao*) of military management is to effect a unified standard of courage. The principle of exploiting terrain is to get value from the soft as well as the hard. Thus the expert in using the military leads his

得益彰，才符合作战地形的规律。所以善于用兵的人，能使士兵协作得像使用一个人一样，是因为迫不得已。

6. 将军之事，静以幽，正以治，能愚士卒之耳目，使之无知；易其事，革其谋，使（人）〔民〕无识；易其居，迂其途，使（人）〔民〕不得虑。帅与之期，如登高而去其梯，帅与之深入诸侯之地，而发其机。若驱群羊，驱而往，驱而来，莫知所之。聚三军之众，投之于险，此将军之事也。

　　将军带兵，要显得冷静沉稳，高深莫测，端庄持重，有条不紊，能够蒙蔽士兵的耳目，使他们毫无所知；经常变换任务，改动计划，使士兵什么也搞不清；经常变换宿营地，做迂回行军，使士兵什么也没法想。将帅与他们约期会战，好比登高而抽去其梯；将帅与他们深入他国领土，然后才披露意图，下令作战。就好像驱赶羊群，赶过来，赶过去，不知道要到何处去。集合三军士兵，把他们投入危险的境地，这正是将军带兵的诀窍。

7. 九地之变，屈伸之利，人情之理，不可不察也。

　　九地的变化，变通的好处，心理的规律，不可不加以了解。

Chapter 11: The Nine Kinds of Terrain

legions as though he were leading one person by the hand. The person cannot but follow.

6. As for the urgent business of the commander:

He is calm and remote, correct and disciplined. He is able to blinker the ears and eyes of his officers and men, and to keep people ignorant. He makes changes in his arrangements and alters his plans, keeping people in the dark. He changes his camp, and takes circuitous routes, keeping people from anticipating him. On the day he leads his troops into battle, it is like climbing up high and throwing away the ladder. He leads his troops deep into the territory of the neighboring states and releases the trigger. Like herding a flock of sheep, he drives them this way and that, so no one knows where they are going. He assembles the rank and file of his armies, and throws them into danger.

This then is the urgent business of the commander.

7. The measures needed to cope with the nine kinds of terrain, the advantages that can be gained by flexibility in maneuvering the army, and the basic patterns of the human character must all be

九地第十一

8. 凡为客之道，深则专，浅则散。去国越境而师者，绝地也。四通者，衢地也。入深者，重地也，入浅者，轻地也。背固前隘者，围地也。无所往者，死地也。

　　一般进入敌国作战，进入较深则意志专一，进入较浅则意志涣散。离开自己的国土，越过边境到他国作战，叫绝地。四通八达，叫衢地。进入敌境深，叫重地。进入敌境浅，叫轻地。背负险固，前为隘口，叫围地。无路可走，叫死地。

9. 是故散地吾将一其志，轻地吾将使之属，争地吾将趋其后，交地吾将（谨其守）〔固其结〕，衢地吾将（固其结）〔谨其守〕，重地吾将继其食，圮地吾将进其途，围地吾将塞其阙，死地吾将示之以不活。

Chapter 11: The Nine Kinds of Terrain

thoroughly investigated.

8. The general methods of operation (*tao*) for invading forces are:

   The deeper you penetrate into enemy territory, the greater the cohesion of your troops; the more shallow the penetration, the more easily you are scattered. When you quit your own territory and lead your troops across the border, you have entered cut–off terrain. When you are vulnerable on all four sides, you are at a strategically vital intersection. When you have penetrated deep into enemy territory, you are on critical terrain; when you have penetrated only a short distance, you are on marginal terrain. When your back is to heavily secured ground, and you face a narrow defile, you are on terrain vulnerable to ambush. When you have nowhere to turn, you are on terrain with no way out.

9. Therefore, on terrain where the troops are easily scattered, I would work to make them one of purpose; on marginal terrain, I would keep the troops together; on contested terrain, I would pick up the pace of our rear divisions; on intermediate terrain, I would pay particular attention to defense; at a strategically vital

九地第十一

所以散地我将使士兵意志专一，轻地我将使士兵保持行军动作的连续，争地我将迅速迂回敌后，交地我将固守要津，衢地我将慎其守备，重地我将保持粮食的供应，圮地我将进据通道，围地我将自塞生路，死地我将示敌以必死。

10. 故兵之情：围则御，不得已则斗，过则从。

所以士兵的心理是：遭敌围困就会抵抗，势不得已就会拼命，陷入困境太深就会言听计从。

11. 是故不知诸侯之谋者，不能豫交；不知山林、险阻、沮泽之形者，不能行军；不用乡导者，不能得地利。四五者，一不知，非〔霸王〕〔王霸〕之兵也。

所以不知道诸侯的打算，不能预结外交；不熟悉山林、险阻、沼泽等地形，不能行军；不使用向导，不能得地利。诸如此类，只要有一件事未考虑到，就算不上王霸之兵。

Chapter 11: The Nine Kinds of Terrain

intersection, I would make sure of my alliances; on critical terrain, I would maintain a continuous line of provisions; on difficult terrain, I would continue the advance along the road; on terrain vulnerable to ambush, I would block off the paths of access and retreat; on terrain from which there is no way out, I would show our troops my resolve to fight to the death.

10. Thus the psychology of the soldier is:

    Resist when surrounded,

    Fight when you have to,

    And obey orders explicitly when in danger.

11. Unless you know the intentions of the rulers of the neighboring states, you cannot enter into preparatory alliances with them; unless you know the lay of the land (*hsing*) – its mountains and forests, its passes and natural hazards, its wetlands and swamps – you cannot deploy the army on it; unless you can employ local scouts, you cannot turn the terrain to your advantage. If an army is ignorant of even one of these several points, it is not the army of a king or a hegemon.

夫（霸王）〔王霸〕之兵，伐大国，则其众不得聚；威加
于敌，则其交不得合。是故不争天下之交，不养天下之权，
信己之私，威加于敌，故其城可拔，其国可隳。

王霸之兵，攻打大国，则其军队无法征集；施加压力于
敌国，则其外交无法施展。所以不去争取天下的外交，不去
事奉天下的霸权，全凭自己的力量，施加压力于敌国，而可
拔取其城池，堕毁其国都。

12. 施无法之赏，悬无政之令。犯三军之众，若使一人。犯之以
事，勿告以言；犯之以利，勿告以害。投之亡地然后存，陷
之死地然后生。夫众陷于害，然后能为胜败。

施行没有规定的奖赏，下达无须监督的军令。约束三军
之众，如同使用一人。用事情去约束他们，不要用言语申
说；用利益去约束他们，不要告以害处。把他们投入死地，
然后才能找到生路。使士兵陷入困境，然后才能决定胜负。

13. 故为兵之事，在顺详敌之意，并敌一向，千里杀将，是谓巧
能成事。

所以用兵作战，在于摸清敌人的意图，根据敌人的运动

Chapter 11: The Nine Kinds of Terrain

When the army of a king or hegemon attacks a large state, it does not allow the enemy to assemble his forces when it brings its prestige and influence to bear on the enemy, it prevents his allies from joining with him. For this reason, one need not contend for alliances with the other states in the empire or try to promote one's own place vis-à-vis your these states. If you pursue your own program, and bring your prestige and influence to bear on the enemy, you can take his walled cities and lay waste to his state.

12. Confer extraordinary rewards and post extraordinary orders, and you can command the entire army as if it were but one man. Give the troops their charges, but do not reveal your plans; get them to face the dangers, but do not reveal the advantages. Only if you throw them into life-and-death situations will they survive; only if you plunge them into places where there is no way out will they stay alive. Only if the rank and file have plunged into danger can they turn defeat into victory.

13. Therefore, the business of waging war lies in carefully studying the designs of the enemy.

    Focus your strength on the enemy

方向而运动，出兵千里，杀其将军，这就叫用巧妙的方法取得成功。

是故政举之日，夷关折符，无通其使，厉于廊庙之上，以诛其事。敌人开阖，必亟入之，先其所爱，微与之期，践墨随敌，以决战事。是故始如处女，敌人开户；后如脱兔，敌不及拒。

所以当决战前夕，要封锁关口，销毁符节，禁止使节往来，在廊庙之上勉励再三，以责成其事。敌人打开门户，一定要迅速进入，先敌占领要害，暗地寻找战机；步步跟随敌军，进行最后决战。所以开始好像未嫁的姑娘，敌人打开门户；然后却像撒开的兔子，敌人已来不及阻挡。

Chapter 11: The Nine Kinds of Terrain

And you can slay his commander at a thousand *li*.

This is called realizing your objective by your wits and your skill.

For this reason, on the day a declaration of war is made, close off the passes, destroy all instruments of agreement, and forbid any further contact with enemy emissaries. Rehearse your plans thoroughly in the ancestral temple and finalize your strategy. When the enemy gives you the opening, you must rush in on him. Go first for something that he cannot afford to lose, and do not let him know the timing of your attack. Revise your strategy according to the changing posture of the enemy to determine the course and outcome of the battle. For this reason,

At first be like a modest maiden,

And the enemy will open his door;

Afterward be as swift as a scurrying rabbit,

And the enemy will be too late to resist you.

火攻第十二

"火攻",指用火来帮助进攻。

Chapter 12:
Incendiary Attack

火攻第十二

1. 孙子曰：

   凡火攻有五：一曰火人，二曰火积，三曰火辎，四曰火库，五曰火队。

   孙子说：

   一般说火攻有五种：一是"火人"（烧其军队）；二是"火积"（烧其储备）；三是"火辎"（烧其辎重）；四是"火库"（烧其军械仓库）；五是"火队"（烧其冲锋队或攻城地道）。

2. 行火必有因，烟火必素具，发火有时，起火有日。时者，天之燥也；日者，月在箕、壁、翼、轸也。凡此四宿者，风起之日也。

   纵火必须有一定条件，烟火器材必须素有准备。点火要选择季节和日子。季节，要选择气候干燥的时候；日子，要选择月亮行经箕、壁、翼、轸四个星宿的时候。月亮行经这四个星宿时，是风起的日子。

   凡火攻，必因五火之变而应之：火发于内，则早应之于外；火发而其兵静者，待而勿攻。极其火力，可从而从之，不可从则止。火可发于外，无待于内，以时发之。火发上风，无攻下风。昼风久，夜风止。凡军必知五火之变，以数

Chapter 12: Incendiary Attack

1. Master Sun said:

    There are five kinds of incendiary attack: The first is called setting fire to personnel; the second, to scores; the third, to transport vehicles and equipment; the fourth, to munitions; the fifth, to supply installations.

2. In order to use fire there must be some inflammable fuel (*yin*), and such fuel must always be kept in readiness. There are appropriate seasons for using fire, and appropriate days that will help fan the flames. The appropriate season is when the weather is hot and dry; the appropriate days are those when the moon passes through the constellations of the Winnowing Basket, the Wall, the Wings, and the Chariot Platform. Generally these four constellations mark days when the winds rise.

    With the incendiary attack, you must vary your response to the enemy according to (*yin*) the different changes in his situation induced by each of the five kinds of attack. When the fire is set within the enemy's camp, respond from without at the

火攻第十二

守之。

　　凡用火攻，必须根据五种火攻的变化而以兵力去配合。火从里面烧起，则应预先在外面接应；火起之后敌军毫无动静，要静观而勿攻。让火一直烧下去，可以借火势而攻就攻，不能借火势而攻就停止。火也可以从外面烧起，但不可在里面等待。要按照时间点火。火从上风点起，不要在下风进攻。白天风刮得久了，夜晚就会停止。军队必须懂得五种火攻的变化，掌握其分寸。

3. 故以火佐攻者明，以水佐攻者强。水可以绝，不可以夺。

　　所以用水来帮助进攻可以壮大其声势，用火来帮助进攻可以增强其威力。但水只能隔绝敌军，却不能赶走敌军。

4. 夫战胜攻取而不修其功者凶，命曰费留。

　　战必胜、攻必取而不能做到适可而止是很危险的，叫做"费留"（耗费资财，淹留不归）。

　　故曰：明主虑之，良将修之，非利不动，非得不用，非

earliest possible moment. If in spite of the outbreak of fire, the enemy's troops remain calm, bide your time and do not attack. Let the fire reach its height, and if you can follow through, do so. If you cannot, stay where you are. If you are able to raise a fire from outside, do not wait to get inside, but set it when the time is right. If the fire is set from upwind, do not attack from downwind. If the wind blows persistently during the day, it will die down at night. In all cases an army must understand the changes induced by the five kinds of incendiary attack, and make use of logistical calculations to address them.

3. He who uses fire to aid the attack is powerful;

   He who uses water to aid the attack is forceful.

   Water can be used to cut the enemy off,

   But cannot be used to deprive him of his supplies.

4. To be victorious in battle and win the spoils, and yet fail to exploit your achievement, is disastrous. The name for it is wasting resources.

   Thus it is said:

火攻第十二

危不战。

所以说：贤明的君主要慎重考虑这一问题，优秀的将领要认真处理这一问题，没有好处不行动，没有收获不使用，不是危险不决战。

主不可以怒而兴师，将不可以愠而致战，合于利而动，不合于利而止。怒可以复喜，愠可以复说，亡国不可以复存，死者不可以复生。故明主慎之，良将警之，此安国全军之道也。

君主不可以因一时之怒而举兵，将领不可以因一时之怒而出战，合于利而行动，不合于利则停止。愤怒可以重新转为喜悦，但国家灭亡却不能复存，士兵死亡却不能再生。所以贤明的君主对之极为慎重，优秀的将领对之非常警惕，这是保证国家和军队安全的关键。

Chapter 12: Incendiary Attack

The farsighted ruler thinks the situation through carefully;

The good commander exploits it fully.

If there is no advantage, do not move into action;

If there is no gain, do not deploy the troops;

If it is not critical, do not send them into battle.

A ruler cannot mobilize his armies in a rage; a commander cannot incite a battle in the heat of the moment. Move if it is to your advantage; bide your time if it is not. A person in a fit of rage can be restored to good humor and a person in the heat of passion can be restored to good cheer, but a state that has perished cannot be revived, and the dead cannot be brought back to life. Thus the farsighted ruler approaches battle with prudence, and the good commander moves with caution. This is the way (*tao*) to keep the state secure and to preserve the army intact.

用间第十三

　　"用间"，指使用间谍。"间"本指"伺候间隙"，"谍"则指"反报"之人。

Chapter 13:
Using Spies

用间第十三

1. 孙子曰：

凡兴师十万，出征千里，百姓之费，公家之奉，日费千金，内外骚动，怠于道路，不得操事者，七十万家，相守数年，以争一日之胜，而爱爵禄百金，不知敌之情者，不仁之至也，非（人）〔民〕之将也，非主之佐也，非胜之主也。

孙子说：

一般出动一支十万人的军队，千里迢迢出征国外，百姓的花费，国家的供应，每天要花费千金之巨，国内外一片骚动，沿途疲于转输，不能操持生计的人将有七十万家之多。相持数年之久，只是为了夺取最后一天的胜利，而却吝惜爵禄钱财，不能掌握敌情，这种人真是毫无仁爱之心，不配当士兵的统帅，不配当君主的助手，不配当胜利的主宰。

故明君贤将所以动而胜人，成功出于众者，先知也。先知者，不可取于鬼神，不可象于事，不可验于度，必取于人，知敌之情者也。

所以贤明的君主和优秀的将领，他们之所以能够动辄战胜敌人，其成就功业超群拔俗，是出于先知。先知不可从鬼神祈求，不可从象数占卜，也不可从躔度推验，而只能从人的身上得到，即从知道敌情的人的身上得到。

Chapter 13: Using Spies

1. Master Sun said:

   In general, the cost to the people and to the public coffers to mobilize an army of 100,000 and dispatch it on a punitory expedition of a thousand *li* is a thousand pieces of gold per day. There will be upheaval at home and abroad, with people trekking exhausted on the roadways and some 700,000 households kept from their work in the fields. Two sides will quarrel with each other for several years in order to fight a decisive battle on a single day. If, begrudging the outlay of ranks, emoluments, and a hundred pieces of gold, a commander does not know the enemy' situation, his is the height of inhumanity. Such a person is no man's commander, no ruler's counselor, and no master of victory.

   Thus the reason the farsighted ruler and his superior commander conquer the enemy at every move, and achieve successes far beyond the reach of the common crowd, is foreknowledge. Such foreknowledge cannot be had from ghosts and spirits, educed by comparison with past events, or verified by astrological calculations. It must come from people – people who know the enemy's situation.

用间第十三

2. 故用间有五：有因间，有内间，有反间，有死间，有生间。五间俱起，莫知其道，是谓神纪，人君之宝也。

　　所以使用间谍分五种：有因间，有内间，有反间，有死间，有生间。五种间谍一起使用，使人无从了解其奥妙，这就是所谓神妙的道理，君主的法宝。

　　因间者，因其乡人而用之；内间者，因其官人而用之；反间者，因其敌间而用之；死间者，为诳事于外，令吾间知之而传于敌间也；生间者，反报也。

　　因间，是利用敌方的乡野之民作间谍；内间，是利用敌方的官吏作间谍；反间，是利用敌方的间谍作我方间谍；死间，是故意把假情报传到外面，让我方间谍得知而传给敌方间谍；生间，是送回情报的人。

　　故三军之事，莫亲于间，赏莫厚于间，事莫密于间，非圣智不能用间，非仁义不能使间，非微妙不能得间之实。

　　所以三军之事，没有比间谍更值得信赖的了，赏赐没有比间谍更优厚的了，事情没有比间谍更机密的了。不是才智过人不能调遣间谍，不是深仁厚义不能使用间谍，不是神机妙算不能得到真实的情报。

Chapter 13: Using Spies

2. There are five kinds of spies that can be employed: local (*yin*) spies, inside agents, double agents, expendable spies, and unexpendable spies. When the five kinds of spies are all active, and no one knows their methods of operation (*tao*), this is called the imperceptible web, and is the ruler's treasure.

Local spies are the enemy's own countrymen in our employ.

Inside agents are enemy officials we employ.

Double agents are enemy spies who report to our side.

Expendable spies are our own agents who obtain false information we have deliberately leaked to them, and who then pass it on to the enemy spies.

Unexpendable spies are those who return from the enemy camp to report.

Thus, of those close to the army command, no one should have more direct access than spies, no one should be more liberally reward than spies, and no maters should be held in greater secrecy than those concerning spies.

Only the most sagacious ruler is bale to employ spies; only the most humane and just commander is able to put them into service; only the most sensitive and alert person can get the

用间第十三

　　微哉微哉！无所不用间也。间事未发而先闻者，间与所告者皆死。

　　微妙啊微妙，简直没有什么地方不能使用间谍。用间计划尚未付诸实施而预先走露了消息，走露消息的间谍与他所告诉的人都要处死。

　　凡军之所欲击，城之所欲攻，人之所欲杀，必先知其守将、左右、谒者、门者、舍人之姓名，令吾间必索知之。

　　凡是要攻打某个军队，夺取某个城池，刺杀某个人物，一定要预先探知它的驻守将领、左右近臣、谒者、门者、舍人的姓名，命令我方间谍务必刺探清楚。

　　（必索）敌间之来间我者，因而利之，导而舍之，故反间可得而用也；因是而知之，故乡间、内间可得而使也；因是而知之，故死间为诳事，可使告敌；因是而知之，故生间可使如期。五间之事，主必知之，知之必在于反间，故反间不可不厚也。

　　敌方派来刺探我方的间谍，要加以收买利用，引导放归，这样反间就可以为我所用；根据反间的使用情况才能决定，乡间和内间可以被使用；根据乡间和内间的使用情况才

Chapter 13: Using Spies

truth out of spies.

So delicate! So secretive! There is nowhere that you cannot put spies to good use. Where a matter of espionage has been divulged prematurely, both the spy and all those he told should be put to death.

In general terms, whether it is armies we want to attack, walled cities we want to besiege, or persons we want to assassinate, it is necessary to first know the identities of the defending commander, his retainers, counselors, gate officers, and sentries. We must direct our agents to find a way to secure this information for us.

It is necessary to find out who the enemy has sent as agents to spy on us. If we take care of them (*yin*) with generous bribes, win them over and send them back, they can thus be brought into our employ as double agents. On the basis of what we learn from (*yin*) these double agents, we can recruit and employ local and inside spies. Also, from (*yin*) this information we will know what false information to feed our expendable spies to pass on to the enemy. Moreover, on what we know from (*yin*) this same

能决定，可以让死间传出假情报，告给敌人；根据死间的使用情况才能决定，生间可以按期返回。有关这五种间谍的各种事情，国君必须知道，知道这些事情必定取决于反间，所以对反间不可不厚待。

3. 昔殷之兴也，伊挚在夏；周之兴也，吕牙在殷，故明君贤将，能以上智为间者，必成大功。此兵之要，三军所恃而动也。

　　从前殷国的兴起，是因为伊挚在夏国；周国的兴起，是因为吕牙在殷国。所以贤明的君主和优秀的将领，若能凭高超的智慧使用间谍，必定会取得伟大的成功。这是用兵的关键，三军靠它而决定其行动。

Chapter 13: Using Spies

source, our unexpendable spies can complete their assignments according to schedule. The ruler must have full knowledge of the covert operations of these five kinds of spies. And since the key to all intelligence is the double agent, this operative must be treated with the utmost generosity.

3. Of old the rise of the Yin (Shang) dynasty was because of Yi Yan who served the house of Hsia; the rise of the Chou dynasty was because of Lü Ya who served in the house of Shang. Thus only those farsighted rulers and their superior commanders who can get the most intelligent people as their spies are destined to accomplish great things. Intelligence is of the essence in warfare – it is what the armies depend upon in their every move.